Relief

Meters		Feet
3050		10 000
1525		5000
610		2000
305		1000
152.5		500
0	Sea Level	0
52.5		500
525		5000
050		10 000

Below Sea Level

© Copyright by Rand McNally & Co. R.L. 86-S-139

ARCTIC OCEAN

Arctic Circle

ICELAND

Reykjavík
Reykjanes
FONTUR
Eskifjörður

LOFOTEN IS.
Narvik
Kebnekaise 6.926
Hammerfest

N O R W A Y
S W E D E N
F I N L A N D
L A P L A N D

Tórshavn
FAEROE IS. (Den.)

SHETLAND IS. (Br.)
Lerwick

Bergen
Trondheim (Nidaros)
DOVRE FJELL
Glittertind
Sognafjord

Luleå
Torneå
Umeå
Oulu

ORKNEY IS. (Br.)

Stavanger
Kristiansand
Lindesnes
Oslo
Karlstad
Sundsvall

Gävle
Uppsala
Norrköping
STOCKHOLM
Åbo
Turku
HELSINKI
Hangö
Gulf of Finland
Tallinn
ESTONIAN S.S.R.
Tartu

NORTH SEA

HEBRIDES
The Minch
Moray Firth
Aberdeen
Dundee
Edinburgh
Firth of Forth
GRAMPIAN MTS.
SCOTLAND

GLASGOW
BRITISH
NORTHERN IRELAND
Belfast

IRELAND
Galway
Dublin
Cork
Cobh
CAPE CLEAR

UNITED
ISLES
NEWCASTLE
KINGDOM
Carlisle
LEEDS
Kingston upon Hull
MANCHESTER
LIVERPOOL
BIRMINGHAM
Leicester

Álborg
Göteborg
Kattegat
ÖLAND
GOTLAND
Visby

Gulf of Riga
Riga
LATVIAN S.S.R.
Jelgava
Daugavpils
Liepāja
LITHUANIAN S.S.R.
Klaipėda
Kaliningrad R.S.F.S.R.
Kaunas

DENMARK
COPENHAGEN (København)
Malmö
BORNHOLM (Den.)
Kiel
RÜGEN

HAMBURG
Lübeck
Bremen
Hannover
BERLIN
GERMAN DEM. REP.
Magdeburg
Leipzig
Dresden

Grodno
Gdańsk
Szczecin
POLAND
Toruń
Poznań
WARSAW
Białystok
Baranov

ST. GEORGE'S CHANNEL
LANDS END
ISLES OF SCILLY

NETHERLANDS
AMSTERDAM
The Hague
's-Gravenhage
ROTTERDAM
ANTWERP
BELGIUM
LILLE
BRUSSELS
Lux.
LUX.

ESSEN
COLOGNE
Bonn
FED. REP. OF GER.
FRANKFURT a.M.
Mainz
Nürnberg

Łódź
Wrocław
Lublin
KATOWICE
Kraków
Lvov
Drogobych
Iva

English Channel
Str. of Dover
Dover
Calais
Cherbourg
Le Havre
Rouen
Reims
Strasbourg
STUTTGART
MUNICH
PRAGUE
Plzeň
Brno
Ostrava
CZECHOSLOVAKIA
Bratislava

Southampton
Portsmouth
LONDON
Leicester

Brest
Rennes
St. Nazaire
Nantes
La Rochelle
Orléans
PARIS
Tours
Dijon
Clermont-Ferrand
F R A N C E

Lausanne
Geneva
Zürich
Bern
SWITZERLAND
AUSTRIA
VIENNA (Wien)
BUDAPEST
HUNGARY
Szeged

Miskolc
Debrecen
Oradea
Cluj
ROMA
CARPATHIANS

Bay of Biscay
Gironde
Bordeaux
Bayonne
Toulouse
LYON
MASSIF CENTRAL
Mont Blanc 15,781
Grenoble
TURIN
Genoa
MILAN
Venice
Trieste
Maribor
Ljubljana
Zagreb
YUGOSLAVIA
Novi Sad
Subotica
Szeged
Belgrade

C. DE FINISTERRE
La Coruña
El Ferrol
Vigo
Gijón
Oviedo
Santander
CORD. CANTÁBRICA
S. Sebastián
Bilbao
Vitoria
PYRENEES
ANDORRA
Nîmes
MARSEILLE
Nice
MONACO
Toulon
Golfe du Lion
La Spezia
Bologna
Livorno
Florence
Ancona
SAN MARINO
Zadar
Split
Sarajevo

Porto (Oporto)
Coimbra
Valladolid
Salamanca
SIERRA DE GUADARRAMA
Zaragoza
Tarragona
Tortosa
BARCELONA
I T A L Y
Rome (Roma)
Naples (Napoli)
Bari
Brindisi
Dubrovnik
Cetinje
Shkodër
Durrës
Tiranë
Bitola
Skopje
BUCHA

LISBON (Lisboa)
MADRID
S P A I N
Valencia
ISLAS BALEARES
MENORCA
MALLORCA
IBIZA
SARDINIA (It.)
Cagliari
Ajaccio
CORSICA (Fr.)
TYRRHENIAN SEA
Golfo di Taranto
Danube
Sofia
BULG

SIERRA MORENA
Seville
Cádiz
Murcia
Cartagena
SIERRA NEVADA
Málaga
Almería
Gibraltar (Br.)
Ceuta (Sp.)
DEL ALBORÁN
C. DE GATA

GREECE
ATHENS (Athínai)
KÉRKIRA
Thessa

Strait of Gibraltar
Tanger
Tétouan
Algiers (El Djazaïr)
Oran
Bizerte
Palermo
Messina
Rabat
Fès
MEDITERRANEAN SEA
C. SPARTIVENTO
IONIAN

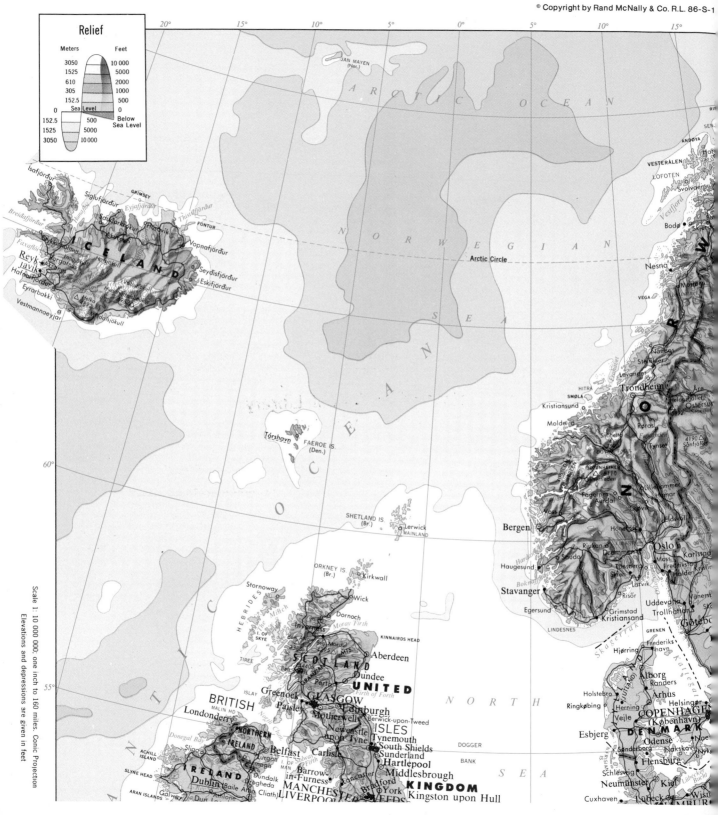

Enchantment of the World

ICELAND

By Emilie U. Lepthien

Consultant for Iceland: Helgi Ágústsson, Minister Counselor, Embassy of Iceland, Washington, D.C.

Consultant for Reading: Robert L. Hillerich, Ph.D., Bowling Green State University, Bowling Green, Ohio

 CHILDRENS PRESS ®
CHICAGO

Vík, a seacoast town in the south

Library of Congress Cataloging-in-Publication Data

Lepthien, Emilie U. (Emilie Utteg).
   Iceland.

   (Enchantment of the world)
   Includes index.
   Summary: Discusses the history, geography, wildlife,
people, social life and customs, religion, economy,
trade, transportation, agriculture, industry, and
culture of the small island nation known as the land
of fire and ice.
   1. Iceland—Juvenile literature. [1. Iceland]
4. Title. II. Series.
DL305.L46   1987   949.1'2   86-29966
ISBN 0-516-02775-1

Childrens Press, Chicago
Copyright ©1987 by Regensteiner Publishing Enterprises, Inc.
All rights reserved. Published simultaneously in Canada.
Printed in the United States of America.
1 2 3 4 5 6 7 8 9 10 R 96 95 94 93 92 91 90 89 88 87

Picture Acknowledgments
© **Bob & Ira Spring:** Pages 4, 34 (top), 73 (left), 86 (top), 99
(top), 104
Tom Stack & Associates: © Keith Murakami: Cover, Pages
5, 51, 94 (bottom), 106; © Brian Parker: Page 20; © Alan G.
Nelson: Pages 42 (left), 105
Root Resources: © Grete Schiodt: Pages 6 (top), 120; © Jane
P. Downton: Pages 8 (right), 10 (bottom), 12 (left), 18
(bottom right), 59; © Evelyn Davidson: Page 15 (right), 107
(bottom left); © Irene E. Hubbell: Pages 49, 103

To the people of Iceland—warm, friendly, hardy, and hardworking

© **Chip & Rosa Maria Peterson:** Pages 6 (bottom), 62, 94
(top), 98 (bottom), 99 (bottom), 100
Third Coast: © Ralf-Finn Hestoft: Pages 8 (left), 24, 39, 96
(bottom), 97 (2 photos), 107 (top left)
© **Sölarfilma, Reykjavík:** Page 10 (top)
© **Lynn M. Stone:** Pages 12 (right), 18 (top), 25 (left), 34
(bottom)
© **Bob Skelly:** Pages 13 (2 photos), 14 (3 photos), 15 (left),
18 (bottom left), 23 (top and bottom left), 25 (right), 26, 32
(2 photos), 42 (right), 46, 53, 56, 60, 63, 66 (bottom), 68
(2 photos), 70 (top), 73 (right), 74 (2 photos), 80 (top), 84,
85 (top and bottom left), 89, 90, 92, 93 (2 photos), 96 (top),
98 (top), 101, 102 (2 photos), 107 (top right), 110
© **Mary Ann Brockman:** Pages 17, 85 (bottom right)
© **H. Armstrong Roberts:** Page 21 (2 photos)
Photri: Pages 23 (bottom right), 52 (left), 54
© **Emilie U. Lepthien:** Pages 27, 28, 50, 52 (right), 61, 64,
65, 70 (bottom), 77, 80 (bottom), 83, 86 (bottom), 88
Historical Pictures Service, Chicago: Pages 31, 37, 41
Icelandic Aluminium Co. Ltd. Page 66 (top)
© **St. Arna Magnussonar, Jóhanna Ólafsd:** Page 78
Courtesy of the Embassy of Iceland, Washington, D.C.:
Page 91
© **Chandler Forman:** Page 107 (bottom right)
Len W. Meents: Maps on pages 95, 100, 103, 104
**Courtesy Flag Research Center, Winchester,
Massachusetts 01890:** Flag on back cover
Cover: View of Reykjavík

A waterfall in the Thjorsardalur area

TABLE OF CONTENTS

Above: A road, called the ring road, makes a complete turn around Iceland, mainly along the coastline. Below: Old lava fields

Chapter 1

ISLAND OF EXTREMES

A large island and a few small islands in the North Atlantic Ocean slightly smaller than the state of Kentucky, Iceland has been called a land of fire and ice: fire because of the volcanoes, and ice because of its glaciers. But Iceland is much more than that. It is a harsh land. It is also a land of the northern lights, beautiful waterfalls, rivers rushing down to the sea, green fields of hay, and moss growing pillow-soft on old lava fields. It is a treeless land with sheep grazing high on mountainsides, and thousands of squawking seabirds nesting in canyon walls. Its seas abound in fish, and seals can be found offshore. It is also a land of erupting volcanoes, spurting geysers, and bubbling mud pots.

Above: Two Icelandic youngsters
Left: A fisherman

THE PEOPLE

Officially called *Lýdveldidh Ísland* (in Icelandic, the name is
spelled *Ísland*), the Republic of Iceland has been settled for more
than eleven hundred years. Iceland's people are warm, friendly,
hardworking, and tenacious. Through the centuries they have
clung to this harsh land, inundated by erupting volcanoes and
washed out in mud slides. Most Icelanders are descendants of
settlers who came from Scandinavian countries, especially
Norway, but there were Celts from Ireland and Scotland also. The
country's rugged terrain has demanded a hardy people, and those
who have stayed—and their sons and daughters and
grandchildren and great-grandchildren—have loved their land.
They are Icelanders and justifiably proud of their heritage.

ICELANDIC SURNAMES

Icelandic names are formed in a unique way. A male's name ends in *sson* or *son* and a female's name ends in *dóttir*. If Stefan has a son named Jon, his full name will be Jon Stefansson. His daughter, named Helga, is Helga Stefansdóttir. When Helga grows up, she might marry Jósef Karlsson but she will still be Helga Stefansdóttir. If Jósef and Helga have children, their sons will have the last name of Jósefsson and the daughters, Jósefsdóttir.

A EUROPEAN NATION

Although this fierce, foreboding island lies just south of the Arctic Circle, Iceland is a European country and belongs to the North Atlantic Treaty Organization (NATO) as well as the Council of Europe and the Nordic Council. Greenland is its nearest neighbor, 180 miles (290 kilometers) across the Denmark Strait to the west. Scotland and Norway lie, respectively, approximately 500 miles (805 kilometers) to the south and 620 miles (998 kilometers) to the east over the open waters of the Atlantic Ocean.

A VOLCANIC LAND

Some countries lie in an area that has a belt of active volcanoes. Iceland is one. The belt runs diagonally through the country from the north to the south, with a side zone on the west and the south. Under this belt is a layer of molten rock that is constantly shifting and all this area is subject to volcanic eruptions. When there are eruptions, disaster can occur.

Above: Hot lava erupting from Mt. Hekla in 1970
Below: Hvannádalshnúkur, Iceland's highest peak

Reykjavík, the capital city, is on the southwest coast. In fact, almost all of the cities, towns, and farms are near the shoreline as the interior is largely uninhabitable. The country is a volcanic plateau; 12 percent is covered by glaciers and 11 percent with lava. Mountains, volcanoes, lakes, hot springs, geysers, mud pots, and glaciers characterize much of the landscape. Icelanders work hard cultivating a portion of the 20 percent of land that is arable along the coastal perimeter.

Hvannádalshnúkur, the highest peak at 6,952 feet (2,119 meters), towers over the land that has an average elevation of 1,500 feet (457 meters) above sea level. Of Iceland's 200 active and dormant volcanoes, at least 30 have contributed to the 150 eruptions recorded since the first settlers arrived. Thousand of acres of grasslands and pasture have been demolished by the smothering flow of lava and ash from these outbursts. Glaciers cover many of the volcanoes, and when those erupt, meltwater floods result. During such an occurrence, the movement of volume of water per second exceeds that of any river on earth. Fertile fields, settlements, and even harbors have been destroyed.

In 1783 Iceland experienced its most calamitous natural disaster with the Laki eruption. Lava flowed down toward the settlements. Sulphuric acid and great volumes of volcanic gasses killed one-fifth of the population and more than half of the livestock. The thirty to forty thousand Icelanders who survived faced starvation. Almost one hundred years later, in 1875, the catastrophic eruption of Askja precipitated a wave of Icelandic emigration to the United States and Canada. But despite the unfortunate historical average of one major volcanic outburst every five years, most Icelanders remain.

Geothermal activity (left) provides energy. It is transported through heavily insulated pipes (right).

THERMAL AND GEOTHERMAL ENERGY

Volcanic activity is not without one important benefit, however. Beneath the volcanic surface lie large thermal areas that can be utilized to provide geothermal energy, a source of heat and electrical power. There is more thermal (relating to natural hot springs) and geothermal (relating to heat of the earth's interior) activity in Iceland than anywhere else in the world. Considering that Iceland is short of other natural energy resources—there are no deposits of coal, petroleum, or natural gas, and no big forests— the presence of geothermal activity and many swift-flowing rivers has enabled the country to heat its buildings and manufacture hydroelectric power. Hydroelectric plants utilizing natural waterpower supply about 33 percent of Iceland's energy needs.

Fourteen high-temperature fields have been located by the

In the high-temperature fields, steam escapes from boiling water (left) and mud pots (right), giving the landscape a science fictionlike atmosphere.

presence of steam holes and bubbling mud pots. Bore holes have been drilled and the geothermal energy obtained is used to generate electricity through steam turbines. Low-temperature areas, characterized by hot springs and geysers, are found throughout the island. The hot water, used for heating homes and outdoor swimming pools, has an average temperature of 167 degrees Fahrenheit (75 degrees Celsius). Eighty percent of the country's homes are heated with thermal energy. Additionally, there is an experimental factory in the Reykjanes high-temperature area where salt is extracted from thermal brine.

   With Iceland's very short growing season, the use of geothermal energy to heat greenhouses is extremely important to fruit and vegetable production. Even hot-weather produce such as grapes and bananas can be raised along with tomatoes, cucumbers, beans, and other fruit and vegetables.

Most fruits, vegetables, and plants
must be grown indoors in
heated greenhouses (above),
but outside geysers spout
boiling water and steam
(below right), and hot springs
(below left) can boil eggs.

Left: The Brull River runs through a canyon of lava beds.
Above: Thingvallavatn, the biggest lake in Iceland

RIVERS AND LAKES

The fast-moving, clear-water rivers flowing continuously over old lava beds not only provide a good source for hydroelectric power production but a splendid source of freshwater fish. Trout and salmon are abundant in these rivers, and in those that drain the old basalt areas, where maximum water flow occurs in late spring. Other rivers are formed by the runoff from melting snow and glaciers, but their waters are murky and contain no fish. None of the rivers is navigable as the currents are too swift and there is too much debris carried along.

Most of Iceland's lakes are small. Two of the most famous are Thingvallavatn, where the outdoor *Althing* (Iceland's parliament or general assembly) sessions were held, and Mývatn. Mývatn is known for its rich bird life, especially the nesting waterfowl, and for its beautiful scenery. Sheer rock walls line the sides of many fjords, while along others stretch narrow rich grasslands where sheep can be seen grazing contentedly beneath the towering cliffs.

THE WEATHER

Iceland, in spite of its name, does not lie in the Arctic Circle— although the northern part is close. On this island of extremes, the weather can change abruptly. Some people have said, "There is no weather in Iceland, only samples." Thunderstorms are rare, although the coastal areas can be very windy. Average temperatures range from fifty degrees Fahrenheit (ten degrees Celsius) in the summer to thirty-four degrees Fahrenheit (one degree Celsius) in the winter. Because a branch of the North Atlantic Drift, a continuation of the Gulf Stream's warm waters, flows clockwise around Iceland's south and west coasts, the country enjoys a milder climate than might be expected from its subarctic location. However, the East Greenland Polar Current passing on the north makes the climate colder in that part of the island in winter. Most of the country enjoys cool summers and relatively mild winters with no wide variation in temperature.

Precipitation varies greatly, however. On Vatnajökull, the largest glacier in Europe, there is usually sufficient snowfall to maintain the size of the glacier. Snow also falls on about one hundred days of the year in the northeast. Inland, however, it is arid. Precipitation is blocked by the mountains on the south coast.

LONG DAYS IN SUMMER

During the summer there is almost continuous daylight. The First Day of Summer, the third Thursday in April, is a public

A panorama of Reykjavík taken at the end of June, just before midnight

holiday. Celebrations are held in Reykjavík and other cities and towns. Actually, summer does not arrive until late in May or early June when the days grow much longer. But the sun is so much appreciated when it can be seen in the fjords, that its appearance is cause for celebration.

Just below the Arctic Circle, midsummer finds Icelanders enjoying more than over twenty hours of daylight. In early spring and late autumn there are long twilights. In midwinter there are only about four hours of daylight. The first day in winter is listed as the third Saturday in October.

Trees are scarce and Iceland is mostly covered with the green of grasses, sedges, and different kinds of low-growing shrubs. The landscape has a unique charm with wildflowers in the geysir area (left), the flowers of the sedge plant (below left), and moss growing on the edge of a glacier (below right).

Chapter 2

ICELAND'S LAND
AND ANIMALS

Through millions of years of volcanic eruptions, the land of what is now Iceland gradually appeared above sea level. Volcanic eruptions continued much as they do at the present time and slowly the island grew.

PLANT LIFE

Iceland's subarctic vegetation includes grasses and sedges (tufted marsh plants) along the extensive bogs and marshes. There are about five hundred species of seed-producing and non seed-producing species of low-growing shrubs. Heather, crowberry, bearberry, willow, and dwarf birch are the most common. Mosses and lichens cover many of the lower-level lava fields.

Eleven centuries ago people first inhabited the island. Large stands of birch trees were cut for building farms and settlements. Sheep were introduced, grazing not only on the grasses but on the small trees. Today, only two small areas of tall birches remain.

The arctic fox was already living in Iceland when the first settlement was made.

In the northeast, south of Egilsstadir, is a national forest that has been protected by the government since 1905. Experimental plantings have been made at this forest station since 1903. Today 50 species of trees from 120 countries, including the United States, Canada, Norway, and Russia, have been planted. It is hoped these trees will survive the Icelandic climate and help to control soil erosion as well as becoming an eventual source of lumber.

ANIMALS

At the time of the first settlements, the only mammal on Iceland was the arctic fox. Foxes still live in the country and may occasionally attack sheep. Visitors often ask where they may see polar bears. Occasionally, a polar bear will appear along the northern shore on drift ice floating down from Greenland, but they are not native to Iceland.

Occasionally polar bears (left) float from Greenland to Iceland on drift ice. These sleeping sea lions (right) live in Icelandic waters.

Along with house and farm animals, the settlers also unintentionally brought mice and rats. About 1930 some farmers imported mink to raise for their fur. Many mink escaped. They have reverted to their wild state and kill many birds and freshwater fish.

Late in the eighteenth century, reindeer were imported from Norway. They are rarely seen, preferring the western highlands.

WHALES AND SEALS

Seventeen species of whales have been found in the seas off the island. Iceland still participates in whaling, but limits have been set by the International Whaling Commission.

The common and gray seal are indigenous, while four other species winter on Iceland. Many seals are killed for their fur

21

during certain times of the year. The fishermen feel that seals devour many of the fish that should be caught and used for human consumption.

BIRDS

More than seventy species of birds nest regularly in Iceland. Seabirds, waterfowl, and waders are the most common indigenous birds. The common eider duck is important to the farmers. They collect the soft down the females use to line their nests, making a soft bed for their eggs and the young when they hatch. Some of the soft eiderdown is used to make warm comforters, but most of the down is exported. Mývatn, a lake in the northern section of the country, is a major nesting area for Iceland's sixteen species of ducks.

The large white-tailed eagle is rare and protected by law. The most important game bird is the rock ptarmigan found in many areas. Ptarmigan is prized on Icelandic dinner tables.

Several species of gulls, starlings, shovelers, tufted ducks, snow buntings, ravens, and wrens are residents, while the swallow, house sparrow, and redwing are summer visitors.

The whooper swan can be found on the lakes near the central highlands. Iceland is one of the few places where the whooper swan is a common breeding bird. Wading birds like the snipe, sandpiper, oystercatcher, and plover are found in shallow water along the coast. The cliffs abound in nesting puffins, kittiwakes, fulmars, and gannets—all seabirds.

Puffins and puffin eggs are favorites on Heimaey, one of the Westmann Islands off the southern coast. They are used for food, but picking puffin eggs is dangerous work. The nests are found in

Iceland is a bird-watcher's paradise. Some of the birds to be seen are puffins (top of page), kittiwakes (left), and plovers (above).

Sport fishermen enjoy the abundance of fish in Iceland's streams and rivers.

ledges on sheer volcanic cliffs. Men dangle from ropes to collect the eggs and run the risk of falling or being attacked by the defensive birds.

INSECTS

Midges, gnats, and flies are the most common of the eight hundred insect species that have been identified so far. Bees and beetles can be found, but there are no ants. Some migratory butterflies arrive in large numbers at times, but they cannot survive Icelandic winters.

FISH

Salmon, trout, char, and eel can be caught in freshwater rivers. Sport fishermen pay very high license fees for one or two days of fishing in the best rivers. The great abundance of fish in Icelandic waters is the result of a rich supply of plankton upon which they

Left: Multi-colored sheep on the island of Heimaey.
Right: Some shearing is still done by hand.

can feed. Even so, various conditions have made it necessary to apply quotas to the amount of certain species that can be caught to preserve the stock. This has seriously affected Iceland's economy since fresh and frozen fish are shipped to the United States and Europe.

Shrimp and lobster (scampi) are found primarily in the northwest and southeast. They, too, are an important source of export income.

DOMESTIC ANIMALS

Sheep have been important to Iceland's economy since the days of the first settlement. They are thick-fleeced, with long outer hairs covering a much softer wool. Icelandic sheep are many colors—white, black, various shades of gray, brown, or mixed or brindled—and it is these natural colors, as well as the softness of the wool, that make Icelandic woolen goods so highly prized. For

Icelandic horses

a country with so few natural resources, wool and woolen products provide a much-needed export commodity.

Both rams and ewes have horns, although those of the rams are much longer and curl several times. The sheep are very surefooted, climbing up over rocky crags with ease as they feed on the mountain grasses or in the meadows. Icelandic sheepdogs are a special breed of dogs that help in herding the sheep. In October they are brought down from the mountainsides. Some are herded into sheep sheds for the winter, where they will feed on hay the farmers harvested in August, and others will be herded down to the shore to feed on kelp, or seaweed, washed in from the ocean.

HORSES

Horses, thought to be descended from Arabian and North African stock, were brought to Iceland in the ninth and tenth centuries by the Norsemen. Through years of selective breeding and life in a colder climate, the Icelandic horse has become smaller than other horses and its coat has gotten heavier. In winter its hair changes color and is shaggy; in summertime, its hair is shorter.

A dairy in Akureyri, Iceland's second-largest town

Historically, horses were the farmer's most valuable animals. The only work animals able to negotiate Iceland's rugged terrain provided transportation, pulled the plows, herded the sheep and cattle, and did the work otherwise performed by oxen elsewhere. Today, although farming and transportation are mechanized and there is less need for the horse, there are over fifty thousand. Many city people belong to riding clubs and most farmers still keep these gentle animals. So special is the breed that the importation of horses from other countries is prohibited.

MILK, PIGS, AND POULTRY

Cattle are raised primarily for their milk. The biggest center of milk production in Iceland is south of Reykjavík. Another center is near Akureyri in the north. Cheese, butter, *skyr* (the national dish, something like yogurt), and pasteurized milk and cream are produced in modern dairies.

There are pigs and poultry, including chickens, ducks, turkeys, and pigeons on farms. Feed for poultry is expensive and must be imported.

Kirkjubaejar, the site where the Irish monks settled

Chapter 3

AN OLD ESTABLISHED LAND

Who discovered Iceland? The writings of the Greek explorer, navigator, and geographer Pytheas mentioned Thule, "the farthest island lying between north and west six days voyage beyond Britain." This was about 300 B.C.

IRISH MONKS

Irish monks thought Thule was Iceland, but Thule probably was not Iceland. Very likely it was some point in Scandinavia. Early in the sixth century, St. Brendan, then an Irish priest, set out with seventeen monks on a holy voyage of forty days. When they reached Iceland they thought they had found Hell. They saw a mountain belching fire, smoke, and hot lava. They imagined that a savage man raced down to the shore flinging hot coals at them. Actually there was no man, but these courageous monks had probably seen an eruption of Mt. Hekla.

"Soldiers of Christ, be strong in faith unfeigned and in armor of the Spirit," St. Brendan shouted to his companions. "We are now in the confines of Hell."

St. Brendan and his companions returned safely to Ireland. Their stories of *Tila*, as they called the island, grew more vivid with each telling. Despite the description of "Hell," Irish monks in later years felt this remote island would offer them a safe haven from invading Vikings.

From 500 to 800 A.D. Ireland was an important seat of Christianity. In its seven kingdoms education was considered more important than personal wealth. The seven kingdoms were joined in two confederacies, one in the north and the other in the south. When fighting between the two confederacies weakened the country, Ireland became an easy prey for Norse invaders, the Vikings. Although the Vikings conquered by the sword, they were also devoted to reason and order. They were not just plunderers. They traded widely where they traveled and their knowledge of various subjects was outstanding. Many Vikings made their homes in Ireland and married Celtic women or took Celtic slaves.

It is thought that the Irish monks fled their homeland and settled on the southern shore of Tila because they felt there they would be safe from Vikings. For many years the monks lived on Iceland undisturbed. (No one knows what eventually happened to the monks, but some think they left when pagan settlers arrived.)

Archaeologists recently discovered what they believe are ruins of a Celtic medieval settlement. Carbon 14 tests seem to date these ruins from about 680 A.D. This would predate any previous records of Celtic monks on the island.

THE VIKINGS

But the Irish monks were not to remain undisturbed. Norse (Viking) sailors voyaged west of Norway to the Shetland Islands by 800. They also settled on the Hebrides, Orkneys, and the Faeroe Islands.

A Viking ship off the coast of Greenland

The *Book of Settlements* (*Landnámabók*) gives credit to Naddoddur as the first Viking to land on Iceland. On a journey from Norway to the Faeroes, his ship was blown off course. He reached the eastern coast of Iceland. Landing at what is now called Reydarfjördur, he climbed a mountain hoping to see some human habitation. Finding none, he and his crew set sail for the Faeroes. A heavy snowstorm fell over the island as they left. Naddoddur named the island *Snaeland* (Snowland). This was about 864.

Gardar Svafarsson, a Swede, might have arrived before Naddoddur according to the *Hauksbók* version of the *Book of Settlements*, compiled early in the twelfth century. On his way to the Hebrides, Gardar was driven west to the east coast of Iceland. He landed on the north coast and built a house at Húsavík (House on the Bay). He named the island Gardarsholmi (Gardar's Island). The next summer he returned to Scandinavia and gave the island high praise.

Glaciers of Iceland, Snaefellsjökull (left) and Vatnajökull (right), add to the stark beauty of the landscape.

Floki Valgerdarson, a Norwegian Viking, heard about the island and decided to settle there. He sailed first to the Shetlands and then on to the Faeroe Islands. From there he and his crew, with a number of livestock, set sail for Iceland.

Like Gardar, Floki sailed down along the south coast, up the west coast, and to the north shore. The men spent their time fishing and sealing in the offshore waters. They did not gather hay from the rich green pastures to feed their cattle in winter. During the cold, dark winter, the cattle perished. The next spring was very cold, too. When Floki climbed a mountain he saw a fjord clogged with ice and a great glacier, Snaefellsjökull, reaching down to the sea. He was too late to set sail for home. Floki had to spend a second winter on the island. The name he gave the land, *Ísland* (Iceland), remains to this day.

THE AGE OF SETTLEMENT

In 874 Ingólfur Arnarson became Iceland's first permanent settler. He settled in a fine, calm harbor. Steam from hot springs rose nearby. Ingólfur called the place *Reykjavík*, Bay of Smoke. Reykjavík became the capital of Iceland a thousand years after he settled there.

The Age of Settlement lasted until 930. Colonization began along the southeast coast although Ingólfur had settled on a bay in the southwest. The grazing lands were good. Forests reached down to the sea. The interior was not habitable then and it remains so today. As news of this land with its rich pastures, forests, and good fishing in the rivers and offshore reached Norway, more settlers came. By 930 most of the coastal areas were claimed.

Many of the leading settlers had been chieftains in Norway and Great Britain. When they settled in Iceland one of their first acts was to construct a temple to their pagan gods. This gave them political as well as religious authority in that area. Some of the settlers were influenced by Christianity, however.

Chieftains were expected to take care of their followers. There was no common law. If a chieftain failed in his obligation, he could lose his power to another chieftain. To solve some of the problems, assemblies called *Things* were arranged in different districts. These were not altogether satisfactory. The Icelanders felt they needed a national assembly.

EARLY TRADE

Being a rather isolated island, Iceland was entirely dependent on ships for its imports and exports. During its first few centuries foreign trade was carried on primarily by Icelanders, who were excellent sailors and owned their own ships. They carried away

In 930 the first Althing met at Thingvellir, now a national park. The priest from the local church (above) is the guardian of the park. An ancient stone wall (below) is one of the remains from the first assembly.

Iceland's exports of dried fish and homespun cloth and returned
with much-needed timber, flour, corn, and iron. However, the
ships were often damaged in raging storms. There were no natural
resources—tall trees or iron—with which to repair them.

THE *ALTHING* ESTABLISHED

About 920, one wise man was sent to Norway to study its laws
and recommend a code of law for the entire island. In 930, when
the first *Althing* met at Thingvellir, Iceland became a
commonwealth. The government of Iceland rested on thirty-six
chieftains. By 965 this had been increased to thirty-nine. There
were two governing bodies: lawmaking and judicial, where
disputes were settled. The Althing is the oldest legislative body in
the world.

The commonwealth was divided into thirteen districts. Each
district had its own Thing. Local Things met in spring and lasted
for four to seven days. Cases that could not be decided at a local
Thing were brought before the Althing, which lasted for two
weeks each summer. Every chieftain was expected to attend.

There was no executive authority. There was no army or police
force. There was no ruler or king. The only official was the law
speaker elected for a three-year term. The law speaker had to
recite the entire body of the law from memory. He had no power
to enforce the law, however.

Each chieftain had to participate in the deliberations and was
required to vote. Then he was expected to explain the reasons for
his vote on every issue.

The Icelandic commonwealth was a democracy. The country
was independent and the Icelandic settlers were proud of their
independence.

STILL INTREPID EXPLORERS

The Vikings had a longing for the sea. They had sailed from their homeland to other countries, generally plundering the lands and taking slaves. When they built their homes on Iceland with its volcanoes and glaciers, the sea still called them. We do not know where they might have sailed after they settled. We do know that they journeyed back and forth to Norway. There was a great need for supplies and Norway, the British Isles, and other countries could provide them with food, timber, and tools.

But they still had that great sense of adventure. It was that desire to explore, to find new land, that led them eventually to North America, to *Vinland*, now thought to be the northern tip of Newfoundland, Canada.

ERIK THE RED

Erik the Red, the red-haired Viking, lived in southwestern Norway. He and his father were forced to leave their home ''because of some killings.'' They fled to Iceland. By the time they arrived around 960, the island was fully settled. The best land had been claimed. But Erik married into a well-to-do family and acquired a large farm in the area of Breidafjördur. He called it Eiriksstadir, naming it after himself. There a son named Leif was born who later became known as Leif the Lucky or Leif Eriksson.

Erik's temper often got him into trouble. After some problem with a neighbor, he was forced to move again. This time he settled on an island in Breidafjördur. After he was accused and convicted of killing the two sons of another farmer, the Thing sentenced him to three years of exile.

An illustration of Erik the Red from a Norwegian saga

GREENLAND'S FIRST EUROPEAN SETTLERS

Erik the Red sailed west to an island. He landed on the southwestern end of the island. There he found green valleys and plenty of fish in the fjord. Erik was satisfied and he selected a choice area for his farm. When his three years of exile were over, he returned to Iceland.

He called the island "Greenland." In the saga written about him he is said to have stated, "people would be more eager to go there if it had a good name."

While Eric was away, there had been a famine in Iceland. In a short time Erik had three hundred people anxious to settle on Greenland. Of the twenty-five ships that set out from Breidafjördur, only fourteen reached Greenland. Several returned to Iceland and some ships were lost in a violent storm.

Nevertheless, two settlements were established. One, the eastern settlement, was around Erik's claim. As first settler, Erik had the authority and the power he desired. The western settlement was farther north on the west coast of Greenland. Eventually there were 190 farms in the eastern settlement and 90 in the western settlement. Between three and four thousand Norsemen finally lived in Greenland. As in Iceland, a Thing was established. Erik the Red was the chieftain.

LEIF THE LUCKY SETS SAIL

Erik's son Leif decided to explore. He bought a ship, hired a crew of thirty-five, and set sail to find lands to the west. Erik himself could have been the leader, but he was getting old and decided to remain in Greenland. His days of exploration had ended, but Leif's had just begun.

On *Markland* (Forest Land), now Labrador, Leif found sandy beaches, flat land, and forests. He also landed on what he called *Heluland*, the south coast of Baffin Island.

Leif continued on and finally, his men discovered a river. They hauled their ship up the river and anchored in a pleasant lake. Fish were plentiful, so they decided to spend the winter there. They built some large houses later called *Leifsbudir* (Leif's Booths). They were built of stone and turf. A kind of awning was used as roofing. They experienced a mild winter without frost.

VINLAND

Leif sent out exploration parties. Tyrkir, a German crewmember, returned to camp babbling one day. He had found grapes growing wild! What a marvelous discovery! Icelanders and Greenlanders had to import wine from the European continent. In

A statue of Leif Eriksson stands in front of Hallgrim's Church in Reykjavík.

spring the ship was loaded with grapes and timber for the return to Greenland. The grapes must have dried and become raisins, but the men had proof of what they had found.

Leif called the land Vinland—Wineland. Later his brothers and other relatives sailed to this new land. Leif encouraged others to go to Vinland. He was willing to lease his "booths," but he would not sell them.

On Iceland's eleven-hundredth anniversary in 1984, the United States presented Iceland with a statue of Leif Eriksson standing in the prow of a Viking ship. It stands overlooking Reykjavík and its harbor. It is a tribute to the brave Norsemen who first ventured to the New World.

BEGINNING OF CHRISTIANITY

While some Icelanders had gone adventuring across the seas to Greenland and Vinland, those on the island had been hearing about some new ideas from Europe. The first Christian missionary in Iceland was called Thorvald the Widely Traveled. He was an Icelander who was converted to Christianity in Germany. He returned to Iceland and began his missionary work in 981. He is still held in great esteem in Iceland.

Other missionaries came, too. King Olaf I Tryggvason of Norway wanted to Christianize all of the Norse settlements. By 1000 many of the leading families in Iceland had adopted Christianity. At the Althing that year, pagan and Christian forces were at odds. The Christians wanted to set up their own commonwealth. They no longer wanted to worship pagan gods. The pagan chieftains did not wish to renounce their ancient gods.

The law speaker at the Althing, Thorgeir Ljosvetningagodi, decided that the whole country should be Christian and the population attending agreed to follow his advice.

CHRISTIANITY IS ESTABLISHED

After the adoption of Christianity at the Althing in 1000, it was not long before two Roman Catholic bishoprics were established. One was settled at Skalholt in the south in 1056 and the second at Holar in the north in 1106.

In a short time the Catholic church became an important factor in the religious and political life of the country. Many young men went to Europe to study for service in the church. Iceland's culture became internationalized in this way.

King Olaf I Tryggvason

Bishop Ogmundur Palsson of Skalholt and Bishop Jón Arason of Holar were the most famous men in the country in the sixteenth century.

THE REFORMATION

In the early sixteenth century, Martin Luther had begun the Reformation in Europe. He broke from the Catholic church and organized his own church. The Danish King Christian III determined in 1537 that Norway and Denmark should become Lutheran. He sent a delegation to Iceland to establish the Lutheran church there, too. A new church code was sent to Iceland from Denmark in 1538. It was not adopted by the Althing until 1541, when two Danish warships arrived with a new Danish governor. The Roman Catholic bishops and clergy were to be removed.

The modern Lutheran church in Akureyri and an old Lutheran church at Glaumbaer

Bishop Palsson was deported to Denmark and died either on the way or soon after he arrived there. Bishop Arason received encouragement from the pope, but the church in Rome was powerless to send him any help. He was virtually under siege.

In 1550, after some success in regaining his former authority, Bishop Arason was seized and taken prisoner. The Danish bailiff had orders to keep him prisoner until the next Althing. However, on November 7, 1550, he was beheaded at Skalholt.

Jón Arason has been a national hero since then. He was beloved by the people who deeply mourned his death. But resistance against the establishment of the Lutheran church was ended. The Danish crown seized the Catholic church properties.

THE STATE CHURCH

Today, Iceland's constitution provides for freedom of religion and worship. The Evangelical Lutheran church is the state church.

The president of Iceland is the supreme authority in the church. Pastors are paid by the government. Many of them serve three or four of the almost three hundred congregations. Over 90 percent of the population claims to be Lutheran. The church no longer plays a principal role in the nation, but the influence of its culture has indeed been great.

THE COMMONWEALTH FALLS

Iceland suffered a number of catastrophies. In 1104 Mt. Hekla erupted, its ash covering half the country. The farms that had been built around its base were buried under 3 feet (.9 meters) of pumice and ash.

By the thirteenth century Iceland had problems. Large sections of land had been cleared of trees and timber was scarce, causing the fleet to decline. Overgrazing from sheep that had been imported had caused soil erosion. There were also political troubles. Six families held the power in Iceland and each one was trying to gain control.

NORWAY TAKES CONTROL

When the problems could not be resolved, the king of Norway, King Haakon IV, was asked to become ruler and to establish law and order. By 1264 the people gave their allegiance to the Norwegian king and they were dependent upon Norway for its trade. In 1349 when the Black Death in Norway took a toll of one-third of Norway's population, trade declined and did not recover. Only one ship entered Icelandic harbors in 1349 and one more in 1350. Finally in 1385 eleven ships came. By that time, many

Icelanders had died of famine. Cattle diseases, storms, and another violent eruption of Mt. Hekla had devastated the island. Hundreds of inhabitants died during a smallpox epidemic. Despite the poor quality of the grain and flour that arrived, trading vessels were eagerly awaited.

Since Christianity had been adopted by the Althing as the national religion in 1000, the church became very powerful under the Norwegian king and archbishop. Chieftains still retained their local authority, however. In 1281, a new code of law had to be accepted by the Althing. Chieftaincies were abolished. The people were required to accept the complete authority of the king. Representatives were sent from Norway to take over the government. The Althing had lost its authority and met very infrequently until 1800. A personal union was established between Norway and Iceland and later between Iceland and Denmark after these countries were united under one king in 1380.

DANISH RULE

In 1380 Norway came under Danish rule. When the Black Death claimed at least one-third of the Icelanders between 1402 and 1404, many farms were idle and fishing decreased. There was nothing to export. Those who survived were in desperate need of imports, especially food.

The Danish government permitted the English and Dutch to trade in Iceland. English traders and fishermen changed the Icelandic economy. By 1413 English ships visited Iceland. Often they came without permission from the Danish king. The price of dried fish doubled, enticing farmers to the fishing villages especially in the south and west. The Dutch also began trading with Iceland. When German traders also sought markets in Iceland, they clashed with the English. So in 1602 the Danish king ordered that his country would have a monopoly on trade with the colony. For a century and a half, Icelanders were forced to trade only with Danish companies. Although they faced famine and starvation, the only flour they could buy was wormy or had mildew. Most of the population lived in poverty. Most turf homes did not have heat and there was little light. The rooms were damp and many people contracted tuberculosis.

In 1855 more than 50 percent of the commercial firms on Iceland were owned by Danish residents. Now all are owned by Icelanders. More than 60 percent of the businesses are in Reykjavík and nearby suburbs and towns.

MORE CALAMITIES

For centuries these conditions continued. In the sixteenth and seventeenth centuries bitter cold killed large numbers of livestock and 9,000 people starved to death. It is a wonder that any people remained on this island. By 1703 the population was 50,444; in 1708 there were 34,000 Icelanders.

In the Laki eruption of 1783, most of the sheep, cattle, and horses died. In the 1784 earthquake in the south, many farms were totally destroyed and over 350 seriously damaged.

BEGINNINGS OF INDEPENDENCE

In 1843 a royal decree reestablished the Althing, mainly through the efforts of the wise Icelandic leader and historian Jón

A statue of
Jón Sigurdsson

Sigurdsson. Twenty representatives chosen by the people, including Jón Sigurdsson, and six appointed by the Danish king met in Reykjavík. The Althing had no power to pass laws. It was merely advisory.

By 1848 Icelanders were demanding home rule. They were allowed to have representation in the Danish Parliament. Slowly economic conditions improved. Increasing numbers of Icelanders engaged in fishing. In April 1854, Icelandic trade became free to all countries. Two and a half centuries of economic oppression ended.

In 1855 Iceland was granted freedom of the press. Nevertheless, without independence many people became disheartened. Many emigrated to the United States, Canada, and Brazil. This continued until the end of the nineteenth century.

THE THOUSANDTH ANNIVERSARY AND A CONSTITUTION

Petitions were sent to Denmark, asking the king for a constitution in honor of Iceland's one thousandth anniversary in 1874. Finally, legislative power was granted to the Althing and self-government was given in domestic affairs. Icelanders were also given control of their country's finances.

King Christian IX came to Iceland in August 1874 to celebrate the anniversary. For Icelanders, too, it was cause for celebration. They had a new constitution.

ICELAND MAKES GREAT PROGRESS

There were many other improvements in Icelandic economic, educational, and political areas. In 1882, a cooperative society was formed. Members could sell their products and buy their supplies through the cooperative societies. It was easier for people to sell what they had raised and cheaper to buy what they needed.

Other institutions were founded in the nineteenth century. In 1818 the National Library was established in Reykjavík. In education, a theological seminary opened in 1847, a medical school in 1876, an agricultural school in 1880, and a navigation college in 1891. The National Bank of Iceland was founded in 1885.

Chapter 4

A MODERN DEMOCRACY

THE ACT OF UNION

Denmark recognized Iceland as a sovereign state under the king of Denmark in 1918 in the Act of Union. This Act of Union was to be in force until 1943 when it would either be revised or ended. There was no doubt Iceland wanted to be independent. But German troops occupied Denmark on April 9, 1940, and Denmark could not fulfill its part of the Act of Union. The next day the Althing passed a resolution giving the Icelandic cabinet the powers of the head of state. In the Act of Union, Denmark had agreed to safeguard Iceland's foreign affairs. With the invasion and occupation of Denmark, Iceland could no longer express its views to the Danish foreign minister. The Althing declared that "for the time being Iceland will take charge of these affairs."

THE ACT OF UNION CANCELLED

The Althing announced on May 17, 1941, that since the country had to take over the conduct of its own affairs, the Act of Union

Iceland's flag

would not be renewed. However, because of World War II, Iceland did not feel it appropriate to formally cancel the union until the end of the war.

INDEPENDENCE

On June 16, 1944, the union was terminated following a plebiscite in which the citizens voted for independence. On June 17, the birthday of Jón Sigurdsson, thousands gathered at Thingvellir, the open-air gathering place of the original Althing, to celebrate the reestablishment of the Republic of Iceland.

Jón Sigurdsson, who died in 1879 at the age of sixty-eight, had been the great leader in the independence movement. Everyone thought it appropriate to honor his memory by choosing that date as the formal birth of the new republic. For seven centuries they had been under the rule of other countries. The red, white, and blue flag they flew was symbolic of the new nation—blue for the sea, white for the glaciers and ice caps, and red for the molten lava.

Freighters and foreign tourist ships dock in Reykjavík

NEW TRADING OPPORTUNITIES

During World War I contacts were made with North American sources for imports of food and other needs. In 1914 the Icelandic Steamship Company took over coastal and transoceanic shipping services. During World War II many ships were lost. A new fleet has since been established. By 1977 the Iceland Shipping Company had twenty-four cargo vessels that sailed to North America and Europe. In addition there are smaller shipping companies that carry exports and imports.

Even so, about half of Iceland's imports and exports are carried on foreign vessels. Ships ply between Icelandic, northeastern European, Canadian, and American ports. A ferryboat operates between East Iceland and the Faeroe Islands, Scotland, and Bergen, Norway.

Keflavík harbor

NATO

In 1949 Iceland became a charter member of NATO. It is the only country in the alliance that is not required to establish its own armed forces. Foreign troops were not to be stationed on the island in peacetime.

In 1951 the government agreed to station a United States defense force at Keflavík, used for observation of the North Altantic Ocean. The Icelandic Defense Force has been maintained by the United States since May 1951.

THE CONSTITUTION

Iceland's current constitution dates formally from June 17, 1944. It has been amended twice, in 1959 and 1968. Much of the constitution is based on the one written in 1944. It begins:

Left: Vigdís Finnbogadóttir, the first woman to be elected a president in Europe, and her daughter
Right: This government office building served as a jail during Danish rule.

"Iceland is a republic with a parliamentary government." It states that legislative authority is vested jointly in the Althing and the president. All elections, national and local, are held by secret ballot. All citizens over the age of twenty have the right to vote.

THE GOVERNMENT

The constitution provides for the election of president every four years. In 1980 Vigdís Finnbogadóttir became the first woman to occupy that position. She was reelected in 1984 and is very beloved by her people. She is the fourth president of the republic.

The cabinet consists of the prime minister and cabinet ministers who serve various departments of government and are the leaders of the administration. The ministers are appointed by the president and approved by the prime minister. Since no one of Iceland's six political parties has had a working majority in the Althing for many years, a coalition of the Progressive and Independence parties is currently in power.

The Althing in Austurvollur Square in Reykjavik

THE ALTHING

The members of the Althing are elected by popular vote for four-year terms. There are sixty members in the United Althing. There are two chambers, the Upper and Lower houses. Twenty members are selected to serve in the Upper House and forty in the Lower. The two houses debate and approve draft statutes. To become law, they must pass three readings in each house.

THE COURTS

The Icelandic court system consists of the Supreme Court and district courts. The six Supreme Court justices are appointed by the president on the advice of the minister of justice.

Appeals go first to the district courts. Each district has a number of district courts. The most important courts are the civil court, criminal court, probate court, court of auctions, and a sheriff's court. Appeals can be sent to the Supreme Court that handles about 150 cases annually. The justices of the Supreme Court are appointed for life.

The interior of the Althing

A labor court for the entire country tries cases involving trade union law. One court has never convened in the eighty years of its existence. It has the power to impeach cabinet ministers.

LOCAL GOVERNMENTS

Not until the middle of the eighteenth century were there any towns. The first town was Reykjavík. It was granted a municipal charter in 1786 and formed a town council in 1836.

Now every town has a town council. Rural districts have a rural district council. Towns elect a mayor every four years. Rural districts have a comparable officer in the chairman of the council.

STATE TAXES

An income tax is collected by the state. Employers contribute to old age and disability insurance, accident, unemployment, and medical insurance. Individuals also contribute to these funds. A church fee is levied on all individuals from age sixteen to sixty-seven. Sales taxes also are collected on goods, with the exception of foodstuffs, and services at the retail or consumers' level.

There are other taxes necessary to support a nation that must import so many things. Since 1982, the value of goods imported has exceeded the export value.

TRADE

Iceland imports goods from at least forty countries. The chief countries from which Iceland imports goods are West Germany, Sweden, Denmark, USSR, The Netherlands, United Kingdom, United States, and Japan. Fish and fish products are Iceland's major exports.

RELATIONS WITH OTHER COUNTRIES

When Iceland became a sovereign state in 1918, neutrality was declared. It has never had a military force or installation of its own. The few ships in its Coast Guard are armed as they patrol the 200-nautical-mile (370-kilometer) fishing limit Iceland claims.

Iceland became a member of the United Nations in 1946. Since then it has joined other international organizations: NATO (1949), the Nordic Council (1952), the General Agreement on Tariffs and Trade (1964), the European Free Trade Association (1970), the Council of Europe (1953), the International Monetary Fund (1945), and the World Bank (1945).

Iceland also participates in various agencies of the United Nations. These include UNESCO, World Health Organization, and the Food and Agricultural Organization.

Twelve countries maintain embassies in Reykjavík. Iceland has either an embassy or consular representatives in 125 countries.

Fishermen unloading their daily catch

Chapter 5

INDUSTRY

How does a country with so few natural resources provide employment and a high standard of living for its people? Icelanders have faced the problem of limited natural resources for 1100 years. And they have met the challenge.

FISHING AND THE FISH INDUSTRY

From the time of the first settlers, the sea has been the country's most important natural resource. For many years, fish products provided the country with 90 percent of its exports. Now it constitutes about 70 percent. Iceland is more dependent upon its fisheries than any independent country in the world.

Because fishing is of major importance to the economy, Iceland has taken measures to protect and conserve their rich fishing grounds. In 1964 the government extended Iceland's territorial waters to 12 nautical miles (22 kilometers), because it was discovered that fish were moving farther away from the coast. In 1972 they extended it to 50 miles (93 kilometers) and in 1975 to 200 miles (370 kilometers).

Government research ships check the available catch of the various restricted species. Iceland's Coast Guard ships make certain that foreign fishing vessels observe the offshore limit, and can arrest vessels fishing illegally in Icelandic waters.

The government's greatest concern has been the protection of the fishing grounds around the coasts. Some countries have disagreed with the limits Iceland set to protect these grounds and that resulted in "Cod Wars" in 1958, 1972, and 1975-76. After the last "Cod War" with Great Britain, an agreement was reached in 1976 and British trawlers no longer exceed the limit.

THE NEED FOR CONSERVATION

The migratory habits of the fish are closely watched by the fishing industry. Meteorologists follow weather patterns, using scout planes and sonar on ships, to assist the fishing fleet in locating large schools of fish. The Maritime Research Institute maintains vessels that survey the potential catch of each commercial fish. More than one hundred species of fish have been caught in Icelandic waters, but most of them have little or no commercial value.

FISH PROCESSING

Drying was the first available means of preserving fish. For hundreds of years dried cod has been shipped to other countries. Stockfish, fish dried without salt, is so thoroughly dehydrated that it keeps a long time in hot climates. Many southern European countries buy stockfish. It is soaked in water, rinsed and reconstituted, and then cooked with spices, herbs, and vegetables.

Drying fish

Salt fish are exported to Spain, Portugal, and Italy. Herring is used primarily for home consumption, although some salted herring is sold to northern European countries and the Soviet Union.

By 1930 iced fresh fish were shipped to Great Britain and Germany. After World War II quick-freezing provided a means of exporting fish over long distances. The fish are filleted, weighed, and packaged before being quick-frozen. Icelandic fish-processing plants have the most modern machinery—descaling machines, fish washers, and other equipment necessary for fish processing— now made in Iceland.

Transporting fresh fish to the processor

"FLYING FISH"

The advent of the jet aircraft enabled fresh fish to be shipped to foreign markets. Boston, New York, Chicago, and San Francisco in the United States receive fresh Icelandic ocean perch, cod, haddock, and halibut carried in the refrigerated holds of jet cargo planes. Luxembourg is the distribution point for fresh fish sent on to other European cities. An Icelandic company is now producing special lightweight polystyrene boxes for transporting fresh fish by air and by road without using refrigerated vehicles.

A NEW SOURCE OF INCOME

Iceland's smallest fishing boats ply the waters close to the northern coast fishing for lumpfish. Only a small quantity of the catch will be eaten. The roe, or fish eggs, are extracted from the fish. Icelandic caviar, as the roe is called, has become an important new product for sale in Europe and American markets.

*Fishermen
checking
and repairing
their nets*

FISH MEAL AND FISH OIL

Capelin is the principal source of fish meal and oil. The entrails of cod, pollock, and plaice also are used to make fish-meal fertilizer. Research is being conducted on the polyunsaturated fats in cod liver oil. Vitamin capsules, providing concentrated medicinal doses, are being produced from the polyunsaturated oils.

SHELLFISH AND CRUSTACEANS

Commercial quantities of scallops are found off the north and west coasts of Iceland. Frozen scallops have found a ready market in the United States. Shrimp fishing and processing are an important source of income to several communities. Lobster, (scampi) too, though harvested on a smaller scale, is gradually growing in importance.

WHALES

Whales provided an important food source for early settlers. Icelanders utilized the entire whale carcass. The meat was processed for human consumption, part was used for pet food and meat extracts, the bones were ground into meal, and the blubber was processed for precious oil used for fuel.

Today whaling is limited to four months. Whalers are forbidden to kill blue whales. To insure whales do not become endangered, the International Whaling Commission has set quotas on the species of whales that Iceland and other countries may catch. Iceland catches whales for research purposes and has agreed to export under 50 percent of the whale meat.

SEAWEED

The unpolluted seas around Iceland are also full of highly nutritive kelp. It is processed into fodder supplements, soil conditioners, health-food additives, and is used in shampoos and cosmetics. Kelp is an excellent dietary source of iodine and some

Iceland depends on fishing and the sea for its economic stability.

other minerals. The western fjords provide a good crop of this pollution-free seaweed, which is harvested and processed within thirty hours. A seaweed extract concentrate is sold to farmers to help rejuvenate the soil. Chemical fertilizers have often reduced the soil's ability to produce crops with high nutritional value.

THE SEA AND ICELAND'S FUTURE

Marine biologists and researchers agree that the sea can no longer sustain unlimited fishing. But Iceland is dependent upon the sea for its economic stability. The need for conservation, quotas, and cooperative management of the sea's resources is apparent.

Preparing fish fillets for packaging and freezing

FISHERIES

The fluctuation in the size of the catch, as set by quotas, or the number of fish available leads to uncertain export income. When other countries provide a subsidy to their fisheries, Icelandic fishermen and processors are at a disadvantage. They cannot compete in price.

On a small scale, fish farming is being undertaken. Salmon and trout are raised on fish farms. Problems have arisen in maintaining the proper water temperature for raising the fish. It is hoped the industry can be developed so it will become profitable.

Icelandair is owned by its employees.

AIR TRAVEL AND TRANSPORT

Air transport began in 1919 when a small plane was purchased for flights within the country. In 1928 an airline company was organized and operated for a few more years. Icelandair (*Flugfelag Íslands*) began international flights in 1938. In 1944 a second company, Icelandic Airlines (*Loftleidir*), also operated within the country. It flew domestic routes until 1952 when it began international service. Internal flights are very important, as large areas of the country are difficult to reach, especially in winter. The road system has many limitations and there are no railroads. In 1973 Icelandair and Icelandic Airlines merged, retaining the name Icelandair. It now carries all domestic and international passengers and cargo.

Above: The Icelandic Aluminum Company at Straumsvík
Below: A hydroelectric power plant at Mývatn

MANUFACTURING

The development of new hydroelectric generating stations enabled Iceland to start building power-intensive industry. The aluminum smelter and ferro-silicon plant use great quantities of electricity, although raw materials for both factories must be imported.

Second in importance only to fish exports is the aluminum produced at the reduction plant in Straumsvík near Reykjavík. Australian bauxite is ground and mixed with a caustic soda solution. After several intermediary steps, the resulting product is aluminum. The aluminum is shipped to harbor silos at Straumsvík, where the Icelandic Aluminum Company uses it to manufacture castings and ingots.

Located in the Hvalfjördur area near Akranes, the ferro-alloy plant needs imported iron and silicon. The new harbor there can accommodate ships carrying five times as much raw material as finished product, a ratio favorable to industrial development. As the demand for ferro-alloys used in the manufacture of steel increases, Iceland's output will become more significant to the national economy.

Many plants utilize hydroelectric power or natural steam to produce fertilizer, concrete blocks, seaweed meal, and sea chemicals. All of these factories use Icelandic raw materials.

The country also manufactures and finds a ready export market for microcomputerized weighing and sorting and other kinds of equipment used by its own fish-processing plants.

Icelandic sweaters and other wool products are well known.
Left: Each part of a sweater is cut out by hand and then
stitched together. Right: A display of Icelandic wool products

PUMICE

Pumice is one of Iceland's few natural resources. Exports go primarily to the Scandinavian countries for the manufacture of aggregate blocks and chimneys. Other countries import it for use in the blue denim industry, where it is used to stone-wash denim clothes to make them look old. The company mining and exporting pumice also exports scoria, a lightweight red lava rock used in landscaping. The United States is the main market for scoria.

WOOL AND WOOL PRODUCTS

Another of Iceland's few natural resources—the marvelous multicolored sheep—provide the justly famous raw wool and yarn that are exported primarily to the United States, Canada, Denmark, and Yugoslavia. Icelandic designers further enhance the natural wool colors with unusual designs in knitwear—both hand- and machine-made—that are eagerly imported by the fashion-conscious United States and western European countries. The Soviet Union also imports Icelandic woolen goods in increasing amounts.

The garment industry has made great strides in design and fashion. The Textile Division of the Technological Institute assists manufacturers in the choice of proper machinery, knitted fabric design, and attention to quality.

FOOD AND FUR

This same natural resource—sheep—even further complements Iceland's economy by being eminently exportable as fresh and frozen lamb and mutton. Dairy products, especially Icelandic cheeses, are sold to many American markets. The sales of soft cheese spreads have grown steadily. Other four-legged natural resources ultimately become—through the tanning industry— lamb and sheepskins, cowhides, and horsehides. The original fox and introduced mink now repay their host country by contributing their fur to a burgeoning business.

CEMENT BLOCKS

The resourceful Icelanders have even adapted the sand, dredged from the bottom of Faxa Bay, to make cement. The plant at Akranes, which produces more than 110,000 tons of Portland cement annually, makes the country self-sufficient in the manufacture of cement blocks for building construction and other uses. With so many large apartment buildings and condominiums under construction, cement blocks are in great demand.

Only about 1 percent
of the land is cultivated.
Left: A farm in the
shadow of a lava mountain
Below: Cutting hay

Chapter 6

AGRICULTURE

Agriculture in Iceland has always been very limited. Only 20 percent of the land is arable. About 1 percent is cultivated, while the rest is used for grazing. The growing season is too short for many crops. At best, only four to five months are available. Most farming is based on the cultivation of hay and grass.

ICELAND'S FARMS

Only about 7 percent of the population is engaged in farming. There are about five thousand farms in Iceland. They are usually far apart. About 90 percent of the farms are independently or privately owned. Some have been in the same family for many generations.

The farmers' principal crop is hay, needed to feed sheep and cattle. Because of the length of summer days and sufficient rainfall, two or three crops of hay can be raised yearly. Cattle require hay and silage for as much as eight months a year and sheep for four or five during the winter. In the spring and autumn, sheep graze on the cultivated fields. In the summer they are moved to the common grazing lands in the uplands and the mountainsides.

CROPS—OUTSIDE AND IN

The cool summers and short growing season prevent farmers from raising most vegetable crops outdoors. Exceptions are potatoes, cabbages, turnips, and rhubarb. In a few protected valleys small quantities of radishes, beets, and onions are grown.

But most of Iceland's vegetables and some fruit are raised in commercial greenhouses. This reduces the amount of these food products that must be imported. In regions where hot springs can be tapped, greenhouses can be heated economically. Hydroelectric power produces the electricity to light them throughout the long winter. The main locale for these buildings is along the south coast in Hveragerdi, which means Garden of Hot Springs.

Icelanders love flowers, and some have small, privately heated thermal greenhouses in which house plants are raised. Housewives enjoy their flowers and plants, often displaying them on their windowsills.

CATTLE

Of course milk production is high. Although there are many dairies throughout the country, including a very large one in Akureyri on the north coast, the main dairy region is near Selfoss in the south.

Icelandic cattle are bred primarily for the milk they will produce. When they are old they are slaughtered. The meat is tough, so it is used for stews or becomes ground beef. About one-fourth of the cattle are raised for beef alone.

Left: Cattle graze not far from a glacier   Right: A Lada, a popular family car

THE MODERN FARM

Today's rural family lives in a comfortable house. Geothermal energy may provide heat. Hydroelectric power brings electricity to light the house and to operate the milking machines, washers and dryers, small appliances, and the television set and radio. The telephone keeps the family in touch with people throughout the island.

Instead of the Icelandic horse, the sixty thousand passenger cars in the towns and cities and on the farms enable people to get together, and make travel and shopping easy. Buses circle the island. Airplanes fly in and out of the country's many airports. There are over 25,000 people living in rural areas and over 241,000 urban dwellers in localities with 200 or more inhabitants. Fewer and fewer people live on farms as Iceland finds itself in its own Industrial Revolution.

The early settlers lived in turf houses (above) and did their cooking over an open fire (below).

Chapter 7

LITERARY TRADITIONS
AND THE ARTS

NORSE: A WORLD LANGUAGE

Many of the Vikings who first settled on Iceland were noble chieftains. When they reached this remote island, they were anxious to have the deeds of their ancestors remembered. They also wanted to preserve their family traditions.

The Vikings had raided the Atlantic coast of Europe from northern Germany down to Gibraltar on the Mediterranean Sea. They attacked Italy and North Africa. The Vikings traveled to Russia on the Baltic reaching Constantinople and Kiev.

Everywhere they went, these fierce invaders learned much about other people and other countries. Their own culture was enriched. Their Norse language became the "world language" for a time. It was spoken throughout Scandinavia, in England, Scotland, France, and Germany. Called Old Norse, it is the language still spoken in Iceland today and called Icelandic.

The Norse chieftains were also religious leaders and built temples at their new settlements. The term for chieftain was *godi* (plural, *godar*). The godi maintained the ancestral faith in heathen gods for the people in his territory.

Each godi was required to attend the Althing after its establishment in 930. The yearly meeting was not only a political but a social event. The old poems and stories were told and retold. The sagas, long family tales, were given orally two centuries before they were written down. Young poets presented their efforts to be judged by their elders. A literary education was considered as important as athletic ability. Contests of physical skill were also a part of Althing activities. But a young noble's ability to compose poetry was as respected as his athletic skills.

EARLY LITERATURE

The sagas composed during the commonwealth's first century related events of that period. Saga means "something said." The sagas of Icelanders tell about persons who lived during that period (930-1030). They record feuds, quarrels, love stories, legends, and events in the lives of families.

The first Icelandic poet was Egill Skallgrímsson. Egill made four trips abroad. His poetry was the first to use rhyme. He was a pioneer in Icelandic literary art.

In *Skaldatal*, a list of Scandinavian and Icelandic court poets (called *skalds*), over one hundred Icelandic poets who reached their peak in the eleventh century were recorded. In their poetry they preserved history, legends, and mythology.

Ari Thorgilsson, who lived from about 1068 to 1148, wrote *Íslendingabók* (*The Book of the Icelanders*). It was a short history of his country from approximately 870 to 1118. He is thought to have written *Landnámabók* (*Book of Settlements*), which gives the names and short biographies of over four hundred settlers.

A statue of Snorri Sturluson stands in Reykholt.

Snorri Sturluson, who lived from 1179 to 1241, is Iceland's most famous author. He composed *Snorri's Edda*, which became a textbook on poetry for young poets to study. Its second section is called "Language of Poetry." A large number of copies of his edda were made for student use.

Snorri was elected law speaker of the Althing from 1215 to 1218. Then he sailed for Norway. When he returned he again served as law speaker from 1222 to 1231. He was the most powerful and richest person in Iceland. It was during the fifteen years from 1220 to 1235 in Snorri's tumultuous life that he produced his great literary works. Among his writings is *Heimskringla*, a history of Norway's kings and mythology, which includes the saga of St. Olaf (Olaf Haraldsson).

Other Icelandic verse was also composed. The verses were of Scandinavian origin. They were the so-called *scaldic* poems. These verses were not collected in a single manuscript. They have been preserved, however, as occasional verses in the *Sagas of Icelanders*.

ICELANDIC BOOKS

The poems and sagas were copied on vellum. Icelanders could read and write. Many people made their own copies of manuscripts. Some wealthy people employed skilled copyists to do the work. Often a space was left for the initial letter to be illustrated. On large vellum sheets the work was copied in two columns. Smaller sheets were made into books.

Árni Magnússon, an Icelander and a professor at the University of Copenhagen, traveled around Iceland for several years. He collected many vellum manuscripts and brought them to Copenhagen. In the great fire in Copenhagen in 1728, many printed manuscripts were lost. He rescued almost all of those on vellum. Árni left all of his manuscripts to the University of Copenhagen at his death in 1730.

Under an agreement between the Icelandic and Danish governments, priceless manuscripts were returned to their country of origin. The first two manuscripts arrived in 1971 from the Royal Library in Copenhagen. Together with other manuscripts they are studied at the Arnamagean Institute in the Arnagardur Museum in Reykjavík, named in honor of the collector, Árni Magnússon.

Opposite page: A manuscript page from Snorri's Edda

Icelanders are voracious readers. The National Library in
Reykjavík (below) was established in 1818. A small section
above shows books available on Albert Einstein.

PRINTING COMES TO ICELAND

Bishop Jón Arason brought a printing press to Iceland in 1531. The New Testament in Icelandic was printed in Denmark in 1540. The complete Bible was published in Iceland in 1584.

In the seventeenth century, 225 books were published in the country, 198 of them printed in Iceland. The people today are avid readers. Half a million books are sold annually in Iceland. Icelanders buy a great many foreign books as well.

FOLKTALES AND MYTHOLOGY

Icelandic folktales include stories of elves, ghosts, mermaids and mermen, sea monsters, and supernatural activities. Superstitions grew from the loneliness of life in a strange landscape, where volcanoes erupted and glacial snow melts buried and transformed familiar landscapes. This was especially true in northern and eastern Iceland.

Norse mythology was written and preserved by the Icelanders. There was a strong belief in spirits and elves. The *Huldufolk* ("hidden people") were—and still are—very real to many people.

Icelandic folklore tells about the origin of the "hidden people." In the Garden of Eden, Eve was bathing her children in a stream when the Lord called. She hid the children she had not washed and showed the Lord the ones who had been bathed. She pretended she had no other children.

The Lord was angry with Eve. He said, "That which is hidden from me shall forever be hidden from men." The "hidden people" are descendents of Eve's unwashed children. They can be seen often in dreams or when they wish to be seen. It is claimed that some Hulddufolk are farmers and shepherds and live like normal human beings. Other people maintain they have seen "hidden people" or played with them as children.

MODERN PROSE

Jón Thóroddsen wrote the first Icelandic novel, *A Boy and a Girl*, while he was a student in Copenhagen in 1850. His second novel was published after his death. Both of his books are classics of Icelandic literature.

By the beginning of the twentieth century there were several new authors. Some were self-educated. They studied the works of foreign authors. One of these was Jon Stefansson. Others received education abroad, such as Jon Trausti (pseudonym of Gudmundur Magnusson) and Einar H. Kvaran.

Some Icelandic authors wrote abroad in Danish or Norwegian. The greatest of these novelists was Gunnar Gunnarsson who won international fame. He wrote many short stories and novels. His finest work was to a great degree autobiographical. It was titled *The Church on the Mountain*. He returned to Iceland when he was fifty years old. He is one of Iceland's most renowned and respected authors.

Kristmann Gudmundsson went to Norway where his first novels were printed. Since his return to Iceland in 1938, he has written in Icelandic. His works have been translated into many languages. One of Iceland's great biographers was Thorbergur Thordarson. His many novels include *Letters to Lara* and *All-too-Wise*.

The Nobel Prize for Literature in 1955 was awarded to Halldór Laxness. His prolific writings include novels, short stories, essays,

Actors portraying Iceland's history

and plays. A new collection of his essays, *And Time Goes By*, was
published in 1985.

Alfrun Gunnlaugsdóttir received the 1985 achievement award
in the arts for her novel, *Wisps*. Indridi Thorsteinsson, Thor
Vilhjalmsson, Arni Bergmann, and Gudbergur Bergsson are
contemporary writers.

THE THEATER

Two theater companies, the Reykjavík Theater and the National
Theater, together give approximately five hundred performances
annually. The People's Theater presents plays especially for
children. The Summer Theater presents "Light Nights" at the
small theater across from Reykjavík's lake. The production in
English acquaints visitors with Icelandic culture.

The Icelandic Dance Company presents classical ballets as well
as dance works created by Icelanders on Icelandic themes.

A free outdoor concert in Reykjavík

MUSIC

Hallgrímur Pétursson's poems have been set to music and are used at religious ceremonies. The national anthem, *Lofsongur*, was composed by Sveinbjorn Sveinbjornsson.

Iceland has a national symphony orchestra, an opera company, and a polyphonic choir. One of Iceland's most famous musician is Russian-born, Vladimir Ashkenazy who is a naturalized citizen.

THE VISUAL ARTS

Asgrimur Jónsson, a nineteenth-century artist, is know for his landscapes. Other prominent Icelandic artists are Johannes Kjarval, Gudmundur Thorsteinsson, Jon Stefansson, Kristin Jonsdóttir, and Juliana Sveinsdóttir.

Iceland's most famous sculptor, Asmundur Sveinsson, created massive statues in concrete that now decorate many public places. His studio garden, which contains many of his works, is now a museum. Other noted sculptors are Gerdur Helgadóttir and Sigurjon Olafsson.

Above: A museum built by the artist features works by Asmundur Sveinsson, Iceland's most famous sculptor/artist. Below left: An outdoor sculpture by Sveinsson is entitled "The Sound of the Sea." Below right: Sveinsson in his garden studio, which is also a museum

Above: An elementary school in Reykjavík
Below: Students gather around their teacher for a lesson

Chapter 8

EVERYDAY LIFE

THE MODERN EDUCATIONAL SYSTEM

Today the country has one of the highest literacy rates in the world—99.9 percent. Education is free at all levels through the university. Textbooks are produced with the cooperation of the ministry of education.

Compulsory education began in 1904 for children aged ten to sixteen. In 1950 school attendance was required for all children from seven up to age sixteen. In many towns a pre-primary education is available for five and six year olds. This provides an important link with the primary school curriculum.

Nurseries are available for children from age three months to six years. Day nurseries have children the entire day, while play-school nurseries have children a half day. There are always more applicants than there are places to fill. In a country where both parents generally work, the nurseries are very important. The nurseries are run by local authorities under the control of the ministry of education. Fees are charged for attendance in a preschool.

The administration building of the University of Iceland, which also contains some classrooms

PRIMARY AND SECONDARY EDUCATION

The school year varies from seven to nine months, depending upon the district. Schools may operate from September 1 through May 31.

Every Icelandic child is required to learn to swim. In a nation where so much of life and industry is dependent upon the sea, this is important.

The comprehensive primary school provides a general education. It teaches students about the occupations available in Iceland and prepares them for enrollment in secondary school. In the last few years of primary school, students study Danish and English along with their other subjects.

Secondary schools are divided into general education, vocational education, or university preparatory. Comprehensive examinations are necessary for admission.

An art class

THE UNIVERSITY

The University of Iceland is located in Reykjavík. The university is an outgrowth of the Theological Seminary founded in 1847, the School of Medicine in 1876, and the School of Law in 1908. They were merged to become the University of Iceland in 1911.

LEISURE ACTIVITIES

Icelanders are avid readers and have a number of libraries available to them, including the National Library in Reykjavík, the University Library, and the Reykjavík City Library and its branches. Many families have personal libraries to keep them occupied during the long winter nights. Iceland is said to have more bookstores for its population than any other country in the world.

A young chess player ponders his next move on a giant outdoor board, while interested spectators observe the game.

About one dozen literary, news, general interest periodicals, and a children's magazine contribute to the reading material available. Reykjavík has over a half dozen daily newspapers. At many bookstores and in hotel shops, magazines from other countries are available.

Television and radio stations are both privately and government-owned. Children's plays, news, dramatic presentations, and some imported documentaries are shown on television.

Foreign movies have been filmed in Iceland and Icelanders have produced a number of films, including two sagas.

Icelanders are excellent chess players. They follow with great interest the championship matches held in other countries. Chess has long been the favorite indoor game. In recent years bridge has gained in popularity.

Íslenska	Jón	Karl
Íslenska járnblendIfélagIð hf	Jón Gunnlaugsson Jörundarholti 154 2329	Karl Ragnarsson Garðabraut 10 1483
Grundartanga (5 línur) 3944	Jón Hálfdánarson eðlisfr Vesturgötu 160 .. 2630	Karl Ragnarsson innrömmun Skólabr 25b . 2497
Eftir lokun skiptiborðs:	Jón Þór Hallsson löggiltur endurskoðandi	Karl Sigurðsson kaupm Dalbraut 27 1870
- Jón Sigurðsson framkvstj 3946	Brekkubraut 29 1026	Karl Sigurðsson vélvirki Einigrund 11 2212
- Stjórnstöð 3948	- skrifstofa 2510	Karl Sigurgeirsson Vallarbraut 17 2821
Íþróttabandalag Akraness Íþróttahúsinu ... 2543	Jón S Hallvarðsson vélv Bjarkargrund 37 .. 1027	Karl Sigurjónsson Garðabraut 24 2848
Íþróttahúsið Vesturgötu 2243	Jón Helgason bifrstj Stekkjarholti 13 1327	Karl Þórðarson Skarðsbraut 11 2474
- Forstöðumaður 2643	Jón Trausti Hervarsson Bjarkargrund 7 1665	Karvel Lindberg Karvelsson
- Jón Gunnlaugsson forstöðvn heima 2329	Jón Hjálmarsson Ásfelli 2279	pípulagningarm Grenigrund 33 2584
Íþróttavöllur Akraness 1216	Jón Hjálmtýsson Höfðabraut 6 2571	Katrín Gísladóttir Mánabraut 3 1304
Jakob Benediktsson hótelstjóri	Jón Hjartarson hárskeri Kirkjubraut 30 2675	Katrín Theódórsdóttir afgrst Höfðabr 14 2710
Laugarbraut 15 2628	Jón Jóhannesson læknir Furugrund 11 2128	Kaupfél Borgfirðinga Kirkjubr 11 ...... 2055, 2280
Jakob Ólason Suðurgötu 39 2694	Jón B Jónsson Grenigrund 24 1231	- Búsáhaldadeild 2034
Jakob Sigurðsson Vesturgötu 37 1376	Jón Magnús Jónsson Reynigrund 5 2524	- Fiskbúð 1351
Jakob Sigtryggsson sjóm Sunnubr 18 2405	Jón S Jónsson Brekkubraut 9 1463	Ketill Bjarnason vélv Grenigrund 8 2361
Jakob Karel Þorvaldsson Jaðarsbraut 17 .. 1060	Jón Skafti Kristjánsson vélstjóri	Ketill Vilbergsson Mánabraut 11 2475
Jakop Hendriksson Vesturgötu 93 1021	Heiðargerði 19 1767	Kiwanisklúbburinn Þyrill Kirkjubraut 11 2005
Janus Bragi Sigurbjörnsson netagerðarm	Jón Leifsson Vesturgötu 101 2714	Kjartan Arnórsson rafvirki Vogabr 58 1077
Vogabraut 24 1669	Jón Leósson Vesturgötu 158 1980	Kjartan Björnsson Akrakoti 2131
Jenný Sveinsdóttir Lerkigrund 1 2523	Jón Magnússon bóndi Hávarðsstöðum 3877	Kjartan Eðvarðsson Vallarbraut 7 1096
Jens Magnússon bifrstj Merkigerði 10 2079	Jón Heiðar Magnússon bifreiðarstj	Kjartan Guðjónsson ferskfiskeftirlitsm
Jódís Pálsdóttir Sóimundarhöfða 1 2136	Bjarkargrund 13 2038	Vogabraut 40 1673
Jóel Þorsteinsson Garðabraut 45 2739	Jón Kr Magnússon bóndi Melaleiti 3840	Kjartan Guðmundsson blikksmiður
Jófríður Jóhannesdóttir Skólabraut 35 2420	Jón B Ólafsson Einigrund 6 2166	Höfðabraut 16 1225
Jóhann Ágústsson Merkigerði 4 2652	Jón Ottesen bóndi Ytra-Hólmi 1212	Kjartan Guðmundsson kennari
Jóhann Ársælsson skipasm Vestur 59a .. 2251	Jón Pálsson vélstjóri Laugarbraut 17 1257	Heiðargerði 5 1582
Jóhann Áskelsson Sandabraut 12 2724	Jón Runólfsson Mánabraut 21 2190	Kjartan Sigurðsson Sandabraut 14 2471
Jóhann Þór Baldursson Einigrund 8 2257	Jón Z Sigríksson Hjarðarholti 18 1314	Knútur Ármann löggiltur rafvirkjam
Jóhann Bogason löggiltur rafvirkjam	Jón Sigurðsson Sandabraut 15 1317	Garðabraut 43 1144
Einigrund 22 1628	Jón Sigurðsson Víðigrund 22 2185	Knútur Bjarnason múraram Stillholti 3 1653
Jóhann Gestsson Einigrund 4 2942	Jón Sigurðsson bifrstj Stóra-Lambhaga II . 3950	Knörr sf Laugarbraut 8 2367

Because so many people have the same surnames, the telephone directory is alphabetized according to first names.

TELEPHONE COMMUNICATION

The telephone is used extensively. Almost every farm, no matter how remote, is linked by telephone. Everyone who has a telephone is listed in the directory by his or her first name, because of the number of similar surnames. The government owns and operates the telephone system.

Iceland is a member of Intelsat, an international communications organization. In May 1983 an Intelsat V (F6) satellite was launched on an Atlas Centaur rocket from Cape Canaveral in the United States. It is located in the Atlantic Ocean region in an orbit synchronized with the earth's rotation, so that it is in a "permanent" position over one point. It carries international telephone, business, and video services. No longer is Iceland an isolated nation with communication dependent upon ships and sailing schedules.

Thermally heated swimming pools are open year round.

SPORTS

Soccer is a popular sport. Matches are held with teams from other countries and some gifted soccer players sign contracts to play with European teams.

Swimming is a popular sport. All students are taught to swim at school. Swimming is available year-round in thermally heated water.

All it takes is a car, a tent, and food, and Icelanders are off on a camping trip. Many groups go camping for the weekends or take their vacation and combine camping with a hiking trip.

Riding horses, golf, sailing, fishing, and hunting are also popular sports. Icelanders also participate in badminton, basketball, handball, judo, and athletic and track events. Skating and skiing are winter sports.

Left: Most Icelanders eat fish at least once a day.   Right: Skyr, *the national dish*

FOOD

Skyr is a national dish made from nonhomogenized milk. It is a favorite dish at breakfast or as a dessert when it is sprinkled with sugar or served with fruit. Skyr, cheese, and yogurt are produced in modern dairies for national consumption. Milk and ice cream are favorites.

For centuries many foods were preserved in sour whey. They included whale meat, lamb fries, and headcheese made from sheeps' heads. Smoked lamb is a traditional dish on Christmas Eve.

Fish is eaten often. Raw pickled salmon is a favorite dish as is herring, used especially in hors d'oeuvres. Lamb or mutton, chicken, and fresh vegetables are a part of Icelandic meals today. Salads are not very common. Sugar is the most used flavoring.

Little is wasted. Fish and meat bones are used for making soup or stock. They are used to make traditional soups. But some unusual soups, such as cocoa or rhubarb, are also popular.

There is no pollution in Reykjavík and on a clear day one can see great distances.
Above: The cathedral dominates the skyline.
Below: The houses, with their brightly colored roofs, look like children's toys.

Chapter 9

A TOUR OF ICELAND

Iceland is a stark, treeless, mountainous country covering 39,800 square miles (103,000 square kilometers). It is a volcanic landscape and the center is a lifeless, barren plateau with glaciers, volcanoes, geysers and hot springs, and lava fields. Most of the population lives in coastal cities.

REYKJAVÍK

Reykjavík, the world's most northerly capital, is located on a fjord, with a modern harbor, on the southwest coast. Snow-capped mountains encircle the city. About half the population of Iceland lives in Reykjavík and its two suburbs; Kópavogur and Hafnarfjördur. As well as being the center of government, Reykjavík is also the artistic, financial, and business center. The city has no pollution, since it is heated with water from nearby hot springs, and as a result is very clean. Houses are built of earthquake-proof concrete blocks painted in pastels and topped with corrugated iron roofs painted in red, blue, and green. Most

Above: The National Museum and Gallery of Iceland in Reykjavík
Below: A park in Harnir

A main street (left) and an open-air market (right) in Reykjavík

houses have their own gardens. Other greenery adorns small parks and squares in the city as well as Lake Tjörnin lying within the city, a lake that is home to swans, ducks, and geese. There also is a river in the eastern section filled with salmon. River Farm is a museum where visitors can learn how the early farmers lived. The Parliament House is a gingerbread Victorian building built in 1881. The graceful Hallgrim's Lutheran Church completed in 1985 has a statue of Leif Eriksson and stands on a hill overlooking the harbor.

Above: A shopping mall in Reykjavík
Below: A fountain in the center of Lake Tjörnin

Above: Apartments constructed of cement blocks
Below: Bankastraeti, the main shopping area in downtown Reykjavík

Strokkur geyser

THINGVELLIR

The site of the original Althing in now a national park with the largest lake in Iceland, Thingvallavatn, which is very cold. Many visitors camp and picnic here among the moss-covered lava rocks, where the speaker's rock and seats for the important chieftains can still be seen.

THE GREAT GEYSIR

The Great Geysir no longer spurts up at regular intervals. The word *geysir* comes from the Icelandic verb *geysa,* which means "to rush forth violently," from which we get the word *geyser.* But

A natural harbor on the beautiful Snuefellsnes Peninsula

there is another geyser, Strokkur, that spouts boiling water about one hundred feet (thirty meters) quite regularly at five-minute intervals.

SNAEFELLSNES PENINSULA

Early Icelanders climbed Snaefell (Snow Mountain) and on a clear day they could see land to the west. The glacier, Snaefellsjökull, covered the extinct volcano. Many years later hardy British climbers ascended "Snow Mountain Glacier" to inspect the crater of the volcano. Their description inspired Jules Verne when he wrote *Journey to the Center of the Earth*. Today's visitors can climb the mountain and enjoy a view of fjords to the west and the sea.

Waterfalls in Iceland are spectacular. Left: Tourists are dwarfed at Dettifoss, Europe's largest waterfall. Right: Gullfoss, the Golden Falls

The loneliest coastal region is Vestfirdir, which juts out into the Greenland Sea on the northwest. The rugged cliffs are a patchwork of snowfields and grassy slopes where sheep graze. Hidden between cliffs is a tiny fishing village, Ísafjördur. Other small fishing villages dot this area and many seabirds make their home here.

WATERFALLS

The most well-known waterfalls are Gullfoss (Golden Falls) where the rushing water roars into a canyon; Dettifoss, Europe's biggest; and the Godafoss (Waterfall of the Gods), the spectacular falls that throw up a spray of water and, if the sun is shining, rainbows appear.

*Panorama of
Akureyri in the north*

AKUREYRI AND THE MÝVATN DISTRICT

Although it isn't very far from the Arctic Circle, the climate
around Akureyri is not harsh. Fertile land contrasts with snow-
capped mountain peaks. Nearby is the volcanic Mývatn district, a
paradise for bird-watchers. In the summer green grass and flowers
cover the lakeshore. Tall mountains composed of ash rise into the
sky amid craters. Namafjöll crater was used as a training ground
for the first Apollo astronauts because its surface is similar to the
moon's. There is also an active geothermal field where pits bubble
up sulfurous material.

Farms nestle in a valley near the glaciers in the southern coast.

THE SOUTHEAST

The greenest section of Iceland is found in the southern coast. There are lava fields, glaciers, cliffs, volcanoes, and waterfalls to explore. Sheep rove the grassy cliffs and the shore is covered with black sand. Here are the glaciers, Mýrdalsjökull and Vatnajökull. Vatnajökull, which covers an area of 3,140 square feet (8,133 square kilometers) and is 3,000 feet (914 meters) thick making it larger than all of Continental Europe's glaciers combined, is in Skaftafell National Park. In summer the glaciers are lit by the midnight sun.

East of Vatnajökull is the small town of Höfn on the fjord of Hornafjörd, its black sand beaches jutting out into the sea.

WESTMANN ISLANDS

In January 1973 all the people of Heimaey, the only populated section of the Westmann Islands, had to leave because of a volcanic eruption. The fishing fleet in the harbor safely evacuated

Heimaey is the only populated section of the Westmann Islands.

all of the inhabitants. In July some people returned and eventually they all returned. They have rebuilt and are using the underground heat as a source of energy.

A series of eruptions began on November 14, 1963 in the sea southwest of the Westmann Islands that eventually created an island named Surtsey. It has been declared a sanctuary and scientists are studying and recording the history of the animal, mineral, and vegetable life as it happens.

THE NORTHERN LIGHTS

One of the most spectacular sights for the citizens of Iceland is the *aurora borealis*, or the Northern Lights. These displays of mainly green, but sometimes purple or red, lights in the sky are caused by electrically charged particles from the sun that reach the earth's magnetic field and travel to the poles. When the particles hit atoms and molecules in the earth's atmosphere, auroras are formed by the released energy.

Camping in the rugged countryside is a favorite pastime in Iceland.

THE SPIRIT OF THE ICELANDERS

Over the centuries Icelanders have survived famines, epidemics, volcanic eruptions, earthquakes, and caretaker governments. They are intelligent, independent, and forward-looking people who intend to make a success of their country.

Some common Icelandic geographical terms are incorporated into some place names:

baer	town, farmstead
bakki	bank, ridge
baugur	ring
bru	bridge
dalur	valley
ey	isle
fjördur	firth, inlet, bay, fjord
fljot	stream
flói	bight, bay, marsh
foss	waterfall
hnúker	peak, hill, mountain
ís	ice
jökull	glacier
kvisl	stream
stadur or stadir	place, spot, town
vatn or vötn	lake, river, water
vík	inlet, creek, bay

---

*The Icelandic letter þ translates into a th in English.

MAP KEY

Place	Grid
Akranes	F3
Akureyri	C7
Aldeyjarfoss	D8,9
Arnarfjördur	C2
Asbyrgi	B9
Askja	D9
Bakkafjördur	B11
Bakkaflói	B11
Bakkagerdi	C,D12
Bardarbunga	E8
Bárdardalur	C,D8
Bessastadir	F3
Bildudalur	C2
Blanda	D6
Blönduos	C5
Bolungarvik	B2
Bordeyri	D4
Borgarfjördur	E,F3
Borgarnes	E4
Breidafjördur	D2
Brjánslaekur	C2
Brúarjökull	E9
Budardalur	D4
Budir	E2
Burfell	F6
Dalvik	C7
Dettifoss Selfoss	C9
Djupivogur	C4
Djupivogur	E11
Drangajökull	B3
Drangsnes	C4
Drekagil	D9
Dyngjufjöll	D9
Dyngjujökull	E8,9
Dyrafjördur	C2
Dyrhólaey	H6
Efrinupur	D5
Egilsstadir	D11
Eldey	E5
Eldgjá	G2,3
Eldhraun	F7
Eiríksjökull	G7
Esja	F4
Eskifjördur	D11,12
Eyjabakkajökull	G6
Eyjafjallajökull	E10
Eyjafjördur	G6
Eyrarhakki	B,C7
Eystri-Ranga	G4
Eyvindarstadaheidi	D6
Faxaflói	F2
Eidar	D11
Flatey	D2,3
Flatey	B8
Flateyri	B2
Flúdir	F5
Frostadavatn	F6
Gardabaer	F4
Gerdar	F3
Gerpir	D12
Geysir	F5
Glaumbaer	C2,3
Godafoss	C6
Grenjadarstadur	C5
Grimsey	B2
Grimsstadir	D4
Grimsvötn	E4
Grindavik	D2
Grundarfjördur	C2
Gufudalur	E9
Gullfoss	D4
Hafnir	E2
Hafnarfjördur	F5,6
Hagavatn	F4
Hagi	F5
Hallormsstadur	C,D2
Heimaey	H5
Hekla	D10,11
Hella	G6
Hellissandur	D3
Héradsflói	G5
Herdubreid	E2
Hljódaklettar	C11
Hof	D9
Höfdakaupstadur	C9
Höfn	C10,11
Hofsá	C5
Hofsjökull	F10
Hofsós	C10
Hólar	E7
Hólmavik	C6
Hóp	C6
Hornbjarg	C5
Hornstrandir	B3
Höskuldsstadir	B3
Hrafnseyri	C2
Hrisey	C7
Húnaflói	C5
Húsavik	B8
Hvalfjördur	F4
Hvammstangi	D5
Hvammur	C6
Hvannadalshnúkur	F,G9
Hveragerdi	G4
Hveravellir	E6
Hverfell	E4
Hvitá	F5
Hvitárvatn	C6
Hvolsvöllur	C8
Ingólfshöfdi	C7
Isafjardardjúp	C8
Isafjördur	A7
Jarlhettur	C10
Jökulfirdir	F8
Jökulsa á Brú	G3
Jökulsá á Dal	E2
Jökulsá á Fjöllum	C3
Jökulsá i Lóni	F5,6
Kaldakvisl	F4
Kaldidalur	F5
Káldranes	C,D2
Kálfafellsstadur	H5
Katla	D10,11
Kerid	G6
Keflavik	D3
Kerlingarfjöll	G5
Kirkjubaejarklaustur	E2
Kirkjuból	C11
Kjölur	D9
Kleifarvatn	C9
Kolbeinsstadir	C10,11
Kópasker	C5
Kópavogur	F10
Krafla	C10
Krisuvik	E7
Króksfjardarnes	C6
Kverkfjöll	C6
Lagarfljót	C5
Lakagigar	B3
Landmannalaugar	B3
Langjökull	C5
Látrabjarg	C,D1
Laugarvatn	F5
Leirhnúkur	C8
Skjaldbreidur	D11
Skjálfandafljöt	G6
Skjálfandi	G7,8
Skútustadir	D7
Snaefell	D9
Snaefellsjökull	F4
Sog	C7
Sprengisandur	G6
Stadarbakki	H7
Stadarsandur	C9
Stadastadur	C9
Stadur	D,E3
Stadur	C3
Stadur	D12
Stokkseyri	G3
Stöng	E5
Straumnes	E4
Stykkishólmur	B4
Súdavik	A11
Sudureyri	G8
Surtsey	D8,9
Svalbard	B7
Thingeyri*	E5
Thingvallavatn*	B7
Thingvellir*	E2
Thistilfjördur*	G4
Thjórsá*	F9
Thórisjökull*	B9
Thórisvatn*	C1,2
Thorlákshöfn*	D4
Thórshöfn*	B10
Thórsmörk*	D3
Thvera*	E4
Thykkvibaer*	F3,4
Tindfjallajökull	C9
Tjörn	G3
Torfajökull	F3
Trölladyngja	C,D1,2
Tungnafellsjökull	C6
Vaglaskögur	G4,5
Varmahlid	F3,4
Vatnajökull	D12
Vatneyri	B7
Vatnsfjördur	F7
Vestmannaeyjar	F8,9
Vesturhópshólar	B,C6
Vík	F5
Vogar	D3
Vopnafjördur	G9
Ytri-Rangá	G8,9

ICELAND

LANDMÆLINGAR ÍSLANDS
COPYRIGHT ICELAND GEODETIC SURVEY

MINI-FACTS AT A GLANCE

GENERAL INFORMATION

Official Name: Lýdveldidh Ísland (Republic of Iceland)

Capital: Reykjavík

Official Language: Icelandic—the oldest modern language in Europe. It was spoken throughout the whole of Scandinavia, the British Isles, and Northern Germany about the time Iceland was settled. Danish and English are taught as compulsory languages in schools.

Government: The government is a republic. The people elect a president who serves for four years. The official head of state, the president, has little power. The government is actually directed by the prime minister, who, together with the Cabinet, proposes and carries out government policies.

The *Althing* (Parliament) passes laws for the country. Forty-nine members are elected directly, and eleven more seats are divided equally among the political parties—the Independence, Social Democratic, People's Alliance, Progressive, and Liberal and Leftist Union parties. Local governments handle welfare, education, health, roads, and law-enforcement programs.

National Song: *"Lofsongur"* ("Oh, Iceland's God, Our Country's God"), words by Matthias Jochumsson, music by Sveinbjorn Sveinbjornsson

Flag: Adopted in 1915, the flag is a red cross, banded in white, on a blue field. The cross stands for Iceland's part in the Scandinavian cultural area.

Money: The basic monetary unit in Iceland is the krona. In October 1986, 40.460 kronur were equal to one U.S. dollar.

Weights and Measures: Iceland uses the metric system.

Population: Estimated 1986 population—245,000; distribution 89 percent urban, 11 percent rural

Opposite page: As glaciers slowly advance and recede, boulders are crushed.

Major Cities:

Reykjavík 87,106
Kópavogur 14,433
Akureyri 13,742
Hafnarfjördur 12,700
(Population based on 1983 census)

Religion: Most Icelanders belong to the state church, the Evangelical Lutheran church. Some belong to the Lutheran Free church, and a few belong to the Protestant churches or to the Roman Catholic church.

GEOGRAPHY

Highest Point: Hvannádalshnúkur, 6,952 ft. (2,119 m) above sea level

Lowest Point: Sea level

Coastline: 1,243 mi. (2,000 km)

Geysers: The word *geyser* is derived from the name of Iceland's best-known hot spring, Geysir. It is of the spouting type, but only spouts irregularly. Another geyser located in the geysir area in the south is Strokkur.
The largest hot spring in Iceland and probably in the world is called Deildartunguhver. It yields 66 gal. (250 l) per second of boiling water, which is used to heat the houses in Akranes and Borgarnes.

Glaciers: Glaciers cover 12 percent of Iceland's total area. The largest glacier, Vatnajökull, covers 3,140 sq. mi. (8,133 km²) and is as big as all the glaciers in Europe combined.

Volcanoes: Iceland has an average of one eruption every five years. The best-known volcano is Mt. Hekla, which is thought to have erupted at least sixteen times.

Rivers: Water from rainfall and melting glaciers form rushing rivers and beautiful waterfalls. The longest river, Thjórsa, flows 150 mi. (241 m) through southern Iceland.

Climate: Iceland has a maritime climate with cool summers and mild winters, thanks to the Gulf Stream. The average temperature in summer is 54° to 64° F. (12° to 15° C) and in winter a little less than 31° F. (0° C). In most parts of Iceland the seasons with the greatest precipitation are fall and early winter. It is often windy in Iceland. On the whole the weather is quite changeable and depends on the tracks of the atmospheric depressions that cross the North Atlantic.

From the end of May until the beginning of August, tourists may find it difficult to sleep because of the midnight sun. There are nearly twenty-four hours of perpetual daylight. But there is a really dark period from mid-November until the end of January. The Northern Lights often can be seen in the fall and early winter.

Greatest Distances: East to west: 300 mi. (483 km)
North to south: 190 mi. (306 km)

Area: 39,800 sq. mi. (103,000 km²)

NATURE

Trees: Once Iceland was covered with woods, but the forests have almost completely disappeared, and there are many efforts to stop erosion and protect areas from grazing. Moss and grass are more abundant in Iceland, however, than in northern Scandinavia and Greenland. Small tracts of wood also remain in inaccessible places. Trees are being planted in an attempt at reforestation.

Fish: There are about 150 species of fish in Icelandic waters. The most important species are cod (*thorskur*), haddock (*ysa*), trout, salmon, and herring. Other species that are caught in considerable quantities are saithe (*ufsi*), halibut (*luda*), ocean perch, ling (*langa*), and catfish (*steinbitur*).

Birds: Birds of over 250 species have been seen in Iceland at one time or another. It is the individual abundance and tameness of birds that makes Iceland such a paradise for bird-watchers. The birds are unaffected by the activities that take place in more densely populated areas. The most celebrated of all Icelandic birds is the Iceland falcon. Two species of owl inhabit Iceland. Other birds that are prevalent are the golden plover, the whimbrel, common waders such as the snipe, the red-shank, the dunlin, the purple sandpiper, the heron, and the blackbird. Iceland has been known as one of the major breeding haunts of waterfowl in Europe.

Animals: Of wild land mammals only the Arctic fox is native. Mice and rats have accompanied people here, as did recently the mink, which escaped from fur farms and is now a threat to bird life. Reindeer were introduced from Norway in the latter part of the eighteenth century. Seals are found on the coast, and sheep and cattle are an important part of the Icelandic economy.

EVERYDAY LIFE

Food: Icelanders eat more lamb and fish than people in most other countries. Even hot dogs are made of lamb rather than beef or pork. Cod and other salted or dried fish are popular. Blood sausages and boiled sheep's head are favorites. The favorite dessert is *skyr*, which is like yogurt and is made from milk curds.

Housing: Houses were once built of turf and stone in the country and wood in the cities, but now reinforced concrete is used, which can withstand earthquakes and the high winds that are frequent along the coasts. Many people paint the outside of their houses in a pastel color. Most houses in Reykjavík are heated by hot water piped from nearby hot springs. Condominiums are increasing in number.

Holidays:
>January 1, New Year's Day
>Good Friday
>Easter Sunday
>Second day of Easter
>Third Thursday in April, First Day of Summer
>May 1, International Labor Day
>Whitsunday
>Whitmonday
>June 17, National Day
>First Monday in August, Bank Holiday
>December 1, Anniversary of Independence
>December 24-26, Christmas Holidays
>December 31, New Year's Eve

Culture: The sagas composed during the twelfth and thirteenth centuries are an important part of Icelandic culture. They record feuds, quarrels, love stories, legends, and events in the lives of families. The eddas, a form of poetry, provided material from the legends about the gods. The most famous edda was written by Snorri Sturluson and has become a virtual textbook on poetry.

Icelanders are among the most literate people in the world. Half a million books are sold annually. Literary and cultural periodicals and a children's magazine are available. There is interest in music and theater throughout Iceland. Even the smallest communities have music schools and amateur dramatics, and the National Theater, the Reykjavík City Theater, and the Akureyri Theater all employ professional companies. There are choirs active everywhere and a School of Singing in Reykjavík. A newly founded opera in Reykjavík has given very popular performances of favorite works. There is great interest in filmmaking. Visual art and design are flourishing.

Sports and Recreation: Icelanders love sports and swim throughout the year—in indoor pools and in outdoor pools warmed by hot springs. Skiing, wrestling, soccer, handball, and gliding are among the most popular sports, and chess and bridge help to pass some of the long, dark winter hours. Salmon and trout fishing are also enjoyed.

Communication: The government owns and operates the telephone system, which ties the country together in a vast network of over 111,000 telephones. There are two radio channels, one independent and one run by the state, and one television station run by the state. Many TV programs are educational, but entertainment and movies are also offered. Iceland was brought into the international system of communication only in 1962 when the underseas line to Scotland was laid, and in 1963 when Canada and Iceland were similarly linked. This more than anything else has led to a cultural and economic revolution with profound changes in the outlook of the people of Iceland. Reykjavík has about six daily newspapers, with a total circulation of 115,000.

Transportation: There are no railroads. People travel mainly by bus, automobile, and airplane. Travel by air is popular and generally inexpensive, and during the past several years domestic passenger volume has increased. Iceland provides regular service to Europe and North America. Except for main streets in the cities, Iceland's 7,000 mi. (11,265 km) of roads have gravel surfaces. Icelanders own about 100,000 cars and trucks.

Education: Children from seven to fifteen, except those in sparsely populated areas, are required to attend school. In the country children ride buses to schools or attend boarding schools. In some isolated areas teachers travel from farm to farm staying several weeks at each farm to teach the children there. After six years of primary school and three years of general secondary school, children may attend grammar school for four years. All grammar-school students learn at least four languages.

The University of Iceland is located at Reykjavík. There are also teacher training and commercial colleges, a nautical school, a music conservatory, and schools teaching arts and crafts, agriculture, home economics, marine engineering, and nursing.

The literacy rate in Iceland is one of the highest in the world—99 percent. Education is free at all levels. Day nurseries are provided for children from three months to six years—an important asset in a country where most women work.

Health: Icelanders have the longest life expectancy of any country in the world: 73.9 for men and 80.5 for women. A healthy diet, which includes many home-grown vegetables, proper immunization, and a high level of physical activity are important factors.

ECONOMY AND INDUSTRY

Agriculture: sheep, cattle, hay, market gardening
Fishing: cod, herring, haddock, salmon, trout, shellfish
Manufacturing and Processing: food processing, metal products, clothing, woodworking, painting and bookbinding, tanning

IMPORTANT DATES

874-920—Scandinavian (Norwegian, Swedish, Danish) and Celtic (Irish) settlers come to Iceland. The first settler, Norwegian Ingolfur Arnarson, makes his home in what is now Reykjavík

930—Establishment of the *Althing* at Thingvellir—the first time a whole nation in one country is ruled by one national assembly

982—Erik the Red discovers Greenland

1000—The Icelander Leif (The Lucky) Eriksson discovers America; Iceland adopts Christianity

930-1262—The commonwealth, a kind of federation of states with a common legislative authority, the Althing, is established, but with district government and executive power in the hands of the local chieftains

1200-1300—Icelandic sagas, the famous medieval works of literature, are written in the Saga Age

1262-1944—Iceland is subject to the king of Norway and, later, the king of Denmark

1281—Iceland adopts new code of law

1380—Iceland and Norway unite with Denmark

1550—Lutheran religion forced on Icelanders; Bishop Jón Arason is killed

1602—Denmark establishes a commercial monopoly

1662—Absolute monarchy of the Danish king is forced upon Icelanders

1783—Laki volcano erupts

1787—Danish trade monopoly is lifted

Eighteenth century—Population decreases greatly due to epidemics and famine

1800—Althing is dissolved

1843—Reestablishment of the Althing

1874—Iceland receives constitution and control of its own finances from Danish king

1875—Eruption of Askja

1903—Iceland received home rule

1911—University of Iceland established

1918—On December 1, Iceland acquires sovereignty, but in royal union with Denmark

1944—Iceland is declared an independent republic on June 17, and an Icelandic president, Sveinn Bjornsson, is elected; new constitution adopted

1945—Icelandic aircraft makes first international flight

1946—Iceland joins United Nations

1949—Iceland is a founding member of the North Atlantic Treaty Organization, the only member of the alliance not required to establish its own armed forces

1951—United States establishes defense force in Iceland

1958—Fishery limits extended to 12 nautical mi. (22 km)

1963—Island of Surtsey develops from volcanic eruption

1970—Iceland becomes member of European Free Trade Association

1972—Fishery limits extended to 50 mi. (93 km)

1973—Volcanic eruption causes great destruction of Heimaey on Westmann Islands; Iceland makes trade agreement with the European Economic Community

1974—Iceland celebrates 1100th anniversary of first settlement; ring road around Iceland is completed

1975—Fishery limits extended to 200 mi. (370 km); Great Britain starts "Cod War" with clashes between Icelandic Coast Guard and Royal Navy frigates, cutting off diplomatic relations between the two countries for a time

1976—Cod War ends with recognition of Iceland's rights and jurisdiction over 200 mi. (370 km) zone

1980—Brief, but intense, eruption starts in Hekla; Vigdís Finnbogadóttir is elected president

1984—Finnbogadóttir is reelected for second four-year term as president

1986—United States President Ronald Reagan and Soviet General Secretary Mikhail Gorbachev meet in Reykjavík

IMPORTANT PEOPLE

Bishop Jón Arason of Hodlar (c. 1484-1550), sixteenth-century clergyman who brought the printing press to Iceland in 1530

Ingólfur Arnarson, first permanent settler in Iceland, A.D. 874

Einar Benediktsson (1864-1940), famous cosmopolitan poet

Sigurbjörn Einarsson (1911-   ), bishop of Iceland from 1958 to 1981

Jon Engilberts, contemporary book illustrator

Vigdís Finnbogadóttir, became first woman president of Iceland in 1980

Agust Gudmundsson, filmmaker whose most famous work is *Golden Sand*

Kristmann Gudmundsson, twentieth-century novelist whose works have been translated into many languages

Tómas Gudmundsson (1901-84), the most accomplished formal master of modern Icelandic poets

Alfrun Gunnlaugsdóttir, winner of the 1985 achievement award in the arts for her novel, *Wisps*

Hannes Hafstein (1861-1922), the first Icelandic minister under home rule in 1904, who wrote visionary poems about Iceland's bright future in a new age

Jonas Hallgrimsson (1807-45), Icelandic national poet; the greatest innovator and most beloved of all Icelandic poets

Gerdur Helgadóttir, contemporary sculptor who works in stained glass

Stefán Íslandi (1907-   ), opera singer

Matthias Jochumsson (1835-1920), one of Iceland's greatest poets, wrote words to national anthem, *"Lofsongur"*

Arngrimur Jónsson (1568-1648), author and scholar, called the Learned, who collected Icelandic manuscripts

Asgrimur Jónsson (1876-1958), Iceland's first artist of renown

Einar Jonsson (1874-1964), sculptor

Hjalmar Jonsson (1796-1875), poet

Johannes Kjarval (1885-1972), master painter whose works have brought high prices

Halldór Laxness (1902-   ), writer of novels and short stories, essays, and plays; winner of the Nobel Prize for Literature in 1955

Thorgeiv Ljosvetninagodi, law-speaker who was instrumental in bringing Christianity to Iceland

Naddoddur, first Viking to land on Iceland, A.D. 864

Árni Magnússon (1663-1730), professor at University of Copenhagen who collected and preserved early Icelandic manuscripts written on vellum

Naddoddur, thought to be the first Viking to land on Iceland

Eggert Olafsson (1726-68), poet and antiquarian

Rognvaldur Olafsson, twentieth-century architect who designed the church at Húsavik

Sigurjon Olafsson, one of Scandinavia's finest sculptors, who did several Danish monuments

Bishop Ogmundur Palsson of Skalholt, famous sixteenth-century clergyman

Hallgrímur Pétursson (1614-74), parish pastor and poet

Gudjon Samuelsson, twentieth-century state architect, designer of many public buildings in Iceland, as well as many hospitals, schools, and churches

Jón Sigurdsson (1811-1879), leader of the independence movement

Egill Skallgrímsson (c.910-990), the greatest of scaldic poetry (occasional verses used in the tenth-century sagas)

David Stefánsson (1895-1964), during the last decades, together with Tómas Gudmundsson, Iceland's greatest contemporary poet

Jon Stefansson (1881-1963), poet

Snorri Sturluson (1179-1241), the most famous Icelandic writer of sagas

Gardar Svafarsson, a Swede who discovered Iceland was an island

Sveinbjorn Sveinbjornsson (1847-1922), composer of music for the national anthem, "Lofsongur"

Juliana Sveinsdóttir, contemporary weaver who uses natural wool colors and Icelandic mountain plants for dyes

Asmundur Sveinsson (1893-   ), creator of massive concrete sculptures

Thorbergur Thordarson, twentieth-century novelist

Ari Thorgilsson (1068-1148), author of *Landnámabók* (*Book of Settlements*) and *Íslendingabók*, a short history of Iceland

Bishop Gudbrandur Thorlaksson of Holar (1541-1627), printer and editor of first Icelandic Bible, 1584

Jón Thóroddsen (1819-68), writer of novels that have become Icelandic classics

Indridi G. Thorsteinsson (1926-   ), novelist, short story writer

Thorvald the Widely Traveled, Icelander of noble birth who was converted to Christianity in Germany

Nina Tryggvadóttir, painter who works in stained glass and mosaic for churches and public buildings

King Olaf I Tryggvason (964-1000), Norwegian who wanted to Christianize all Icelandic settlements

Floki Valgerdarson, a Viking who first called Iceland "Iceland"

Skaftafell National Park

INDEX

Page numbers that appear in boldface type indicate illustrations

About the Author

Emilie Utteg Lepthien earned a BS and MA degree and a certificate in school administration from Northwestern University. She has worked as an upper grade science and social studies teacher supervisor and a principal of an elementary and upper grade center for twenty years. Ms. Lepthien also has written and narrated science and social studies scripts for the Radio Council of the Chicago Board of Education.

Ms. Lepthien was awarded the American Educator's Medal by Freedoms Foundation. She is a member of the Delta Kappa Gamma Society International, Chicago Principals Association and life member of the NEA. She has been a co-author of primary social studies texts for Rand, McNally and Co. and an educational consultant for Encyclopaedia Britannica Films. Ms. Lepthien has written Enchantment of the World books on Australia, Ecuador, and the Philippines.

DATE DUE

Demco, Inc. 38-293